AF596804

E-VOLVEMENT

VOLUME 1

VRIIN C

INDIA • SINGAPORE • MALAYSIA

ISBN 979-8-89322-964-6

Disclaimer

The information provided in this book is for informational purposes only and is not intended as a substitute for professional medical advice, diagnosis, or treatment. The practices and techniques shared are based on personal experiences and research into self-healing methods for emotional & spiritual well-being. Always consult with a qualified healthcare professional before starting any new wellness program, making significant lifestyle changes, or if you have any concerns about your health.

The author and publisher disclaim any liability for any injuries, losses, or damages incurred by the use or reliance on the information in this book. By engaging with this material, you understand and accept that any actions taken by you based on its content are entirely your own responsibility.

Dedications

To my mother Kanwaljit. You saw me not what I was but what I could be. You're my mom, my friend, my healer and my guide always.

To my sister Hashveen. It was your unconditional love that sustained me and made me choose self healing.

To my son Ishpreet. You are my voice of reason, the other half of my soul. You're my biggest blessing.

To my brother Daljeet. Your immense wisdom, your silent love, your subtle hints are the reason this book could be written. I'm not just your sister but your biggest fan.

Cover Art Design created by
Shubham Singhania
The Mooch Studio

Credit for all sketches to Vijay Jitiya and Sonal Jitiya from Fusion Tattoos - An Art Studio
Connect with them on +917506203750.
https://instagram.com/fusion.tattoos

Contents

Part 2

Foreword

E-VOLVEMENT by Vriin C: A Thought-Provoking Journey towards Collective Growth

Thank you, Vriin, for sharing such a wealth of insights and life-changing examples. E-VOLVEMENT is about evolving together and winning in day-to-day life. The writing style creates the impression that the book is speaking directly to the reader. Statements like "Weak souls make weak decisions" provoke deep reflection. Vriin has incorporated a fair amount of research, adding depth to the narrative.

This well-researched book will support your quest to energize your soul and improve your "Happiness Quotient." The book lucidly explores the shifting pace of life in the digital era and the associated challenges, such as work-life balance and the generational gap. It also addresses how external versus internal changes define us.

There is a dedicated chapter titled "What Changed Inside" that delves into the impact of the past. In another chapter, the Author (Vriin) discusses three intriguing leadership qualities: being Earthquake-Proof, Noise-Proof, and Future-Ready. The book further elaborates on the concepts of the three C's and Soul Leadership. The process of Soul Leadership is both fascinating and practical.

The book references ancient scriptures, classical writings, and modern quotes to effectively convey its central ideas. Overall, E-VOLVEMENT is an engaging and insightful read that helps build a perspective for real life, making it a must-read for everyone.

– Alok Sheopurkar - Head HR - HDFC Asset Management Company Limited.

Reviews

The human mind is instinctive. The human soul is ancient. Human technology is modern. The current period in human history is probably the most challenging, but also, potentially the most exciting… for those who know how to navigate this complex landscape and e-volve to the next level. Let Vriin show you how.

– Ron Malhotra (The Indian Lion)
International Speaker, Mentor & one of India's most influential thought leaders of the current decade.

E-volvement resonates deeply with anyone who has ever pondered the "what ifs" of life.

The writing is both relatable and deeply insightful, offering profound yet relatable lessons on finding joy even in the most challenging times. The narrative is engrossing, with a rhythm that pulls you into an emotional journey, making you feel every triumph and setback as if they were your own.

The Author (Vriin) shares her personal stories and experiences, which are not only deeply moving but also resonate at a universal level. Her honest take on suffering, resilience, and the pursuit of happiness make the book a treasure trove of wisdom that can be revisited throughout life.

This book is not just a delightful read but a lifelong companion that offers comfort and guidance whenever needed.

– Sabah Iqbal
Co-Founder - Semeion Consulting

This book takes one seamlessly from the circumstances and beliefs one carries through traditions, upbringing and historical events to the current environment of high competition. It gives light to the essence behind peer pressures and toxic relationships.

E-volvement is key towards self discovery and gaining of self confidence. To employ a balanced approach not just for creating a meaningful life but also at the same time to search within oneself. I felt the E-volvement process defined by the Author (Vriin) also defines the purpose of one's existence and how we can all lead a life drenched in tranquility harmony and at the end making it joyful and fulfilling.

– NR Subramanian
Executive Vice President,
Kotak Commodity Services Private Limited.

Preface

Do not compare yourself to others. Your soul goes through different ages. You can have the soul of a child, an adult or someone old. It takes an old soul to want answers. Wanting to know more is the inherent characteristic of an old soul. From a reactive mode of wanting more, you have now transitioned into the progressive and proactive mode of desiring more. Your desire to learn more about yourself and your relationship with others, the universe, and God has led you to this book.

When I decided to want more from my life in 2001, I was unsure as this was an unknown route for me. I was not satisfied with the narrative imposed on me by others and gathered the courage to follow my path. I could not have predicted where it led me. I knew one thing for sure; I was unsatisfied with my life and there had to be something better out there.

I wasn't sure where I was going and most importantly how I would get there. I just knew that I could no longer exist the way I had to date. I could not be someone whom others could control and make decisions for. I looked hard into the depths of my soul and decided I deserved more. All my experiences and learnings since then have given me a window into a whole new world. They made me see the world not as something physical but as a connected web of energy. This can be compared to radio frequencies. You need to tune into the frequency of your choice to receive the channel you need.

I have chosen to become mentally, emotionally, physically, and financially stronger and become a leader of my own life. I now choose to share my secrets as I believe in the power of giving. Through the three volumes of E-volvement, I would like to empower people in the world and help them take control of their own lives. However, each person undergoes a unique process. Their empowerment will bring them solutions and begin the movement of creating a better world.

It is possible. I can attest to this transformation but also know that this cannot be done in isolation.

Hence, the E-volvement slogan is 'I evolve you. You evolve me. We evolve together.'

You have to start the chain reaction of evolvement. Get the energy flowing. The E in E-volvement is your soul energy. You need to raise this energy to tune into the radio channel of your dreams to become the most successful version of yourself. You need to give unto others so that your community learns from you and you create your heaven.

I have created my heaven and am living a blessed life. I love all my relationships and am achieving more and more each day. I am blissfully happy, contented, and peaceful. My world is filled with laughter and health.

I wish the same for you. Your picking up this book is not a coincidence. The emotions that made you pick up this book are guiding you towards your evolvement.

This is your time.

Awakening

The two most defining moments of my life took place within three months of each other. It would definitely take something big for a shy, obedient, dutiful, and accepting girl in a patriarchal family to stand up for herself and create her own life. However, it was only much later that I correlated these events and realised the impact they had on me. I was able to correlate everything many years later when I was asked to pinpoint the exact moment something changed within me. However, while these events were playing out, I was clueless and confused about my life. But I felt like somewhere a switch was flipped allowing my inner light to shine. It started the chain reaction that led to my awakening.

The event

At the age of 20, I agreed to an arranged marriage and got engaged. This type of marriage is common in Indian society and I believe that it is a good practice. The engagement was called off three weeks before the wedding due to some exigencies, causing extreme tension and distress within my family. We were going through some financial issues at the time and this was perceived as the final straw. Since I did not wish to be a burden on my family, I agreed to another arranged marriage to alleviate their distress. Instead of getting married on the 9th of December 1995, I got married to a different groom on the 28th of January 1996. The problems in my life were not due to this but because of my self-image issues. A more confident person would have enquired more deeply, thought for herself and reserved the right to choose instead of blindly accepting the decisions made by others. The problem lay with my lack of certainty.

I wasn't forced into the arranged marriage. I agreed to it and believed that it was my only choice as I could not perceive any other reality. It was my compliance and acceptance of the status quo that was wrong. I accepted the fact that I had no choice of my own. I gave up the right to choose my own life. I chose to be dependent on my parents and later my husband rather than try to carve my path in the world. I chose to be weak.

How can anyone choose to be weak? What were the factors that made me weak? What other choices could I have made if my soul had been strong? Which path would my life have taken if my soul had been energised or replete and not looking at others for fulfilment? I wish that someone had given me the answers to these questions at the age of 20. I now realise that my parents were not at fault as they were stuck in a loop themselves and had weak souls. They did, however, try their best under the circumstances.

My marriage lasted six years and at the age of 26, I chose to opt out of the disrespectful and soul-depleting union. I chose to raise my son the way I wanted to and finally live life on my terms.

Our decisions create our reality

Weak souls make weak decisions. Powerful and energised souls make life-changing and empowering decisions. A low-wattage light bulb will provide only limited light making it visible only to some. However, a high-wattage one provides everyone around with light. To create a powerful reality, you need to take powerful decisions. To take powerful and impactful decisions, you need to energise your soul and evolve. While the evolvement of mankind has been taking place for many years, you are only just starting the evolvement of your soul. Energise your soul. Everything else will start falling into place. If you do not have enough energy in your soul, you only exist. When you increase the energy of your soul, you start to lead. Compare this to the mobile phone that you are so fond of. It doesn't matter how expensive the phone is or how many apps you have downloaded on it. The performance of your phone depends on whether it is fully charged. Your soul, like your phone, requires energy for charging.

My evolvement towards generating, sustaining and energising my soul was a torturous and long journey. With this book, I hope you can achieve much more than I did and within a much shorter time frame. Also, all of you are learners and have the responsibility to share this learning. I hope my learnings, mentioned in this book, will help you in your evolvement and that you receive many of the answers you seek. In turn, I hope that your answers can be shared with me so I too can learn more and evolve further.

I often refer to the soul and soul energy as I have realised that this is the main ingredient or the missing element that you need to reclaim your life. This element will ensure that all other areas of your life function at the highest potential. This one element will create the change and transformation that you seek to become truly powerful.

I recommend you read this book completely to fully comprehend the nuances of soul energy. However, once done, you can also open random pages to search for your answers. The things shared in this book will help you find your answers as and when you seek them, either now or in the future. This book has been written not by me but through me and you will be amazed at what answers leap out based on where you are in your life.

Introduction

When I look back at my younger self, I wonder what was going through my mind when I took major life decisions with certainty. I also realised something. It's okay to take bad decisions if you learn from them. If you accept them, move on, and definitely do not blame others. The others in your life are themselves stuck in their life patterns and probably aren't aware that these can be broken.

Let's take the example of Ashish. He has been on a 10-day fast. Would you expect him to run a marathon, score a goal, or be as active as his normal self? I don't know about you but I certainly wouldn't. After his prolonged fast, Ashish would need every bit of help to stand up, let alone participate in any physical or mental activities. Can you then blame him for his procrastination, for being lazy and not taking charge of his life? Do you think Ashish should blame himself, feel guilty, and have a never-ending conversation with himself justifying why exactly he has low energy?

What did the lack of food do to him? Lack of food equals lack of sustenance or fuel per se. This fuel is required to charge the brilliant piece of machinery that is your human body. It not only charges your body but also frees you to achieve your other goals. When the body is replenished, you not only focus on the digestive process but also feel renewed and can focus on your daily tasks, goals, and vision. In Ashish's case, being inactive and slow was a natural progression and a direct result of the fast as his body did not receive the sustenance and fuel it needed to function at optimum levels.

I've seen malnutrition in children and adults. Their return to normalcy after treatment takes time. The medics don't start them on a protein and calorie-rich diet immediately. Eating food will make them better but something as basic as the capacity to digest and absorb will also need to be built over time. Don't you agree that the body will need time to regain its capacity to digest food and then convert it into fuel? Recovery is slow. Achieving a healthy body and mind takes days, sometimes months. As you may be well aware, apart from food, the body needs several other factors such as exercise, fresh air and sunlight to generate energy and be active.

I'm sure you are all experts at understanding your own body. While these methods help in looking after the physical body, what about the soul? Is your soul receiving sufficient fuel or sustenance? Is it barely surviving or is it actually blooming?

Do you think your soul is receiving all the energy it requires? Not just to function but to remain energised and prosper. What steps have you taken to ensure your soul energy is charged? What measures have you put in place to ensure your soul energy doesn't get depleted? What was a matter of simply charging your soul has reached an urgent level. You can compare this to your mobile phone when the charge is below 10%. You need to immediately find the nearest charging point and recharge it. Similarly, there is an urgent need to recharge the soul energy to prosper and remain energised.

Would you expect your soul, which has been functioning at the bare minimum levels for the past several years, to have sufficient energy to help you succeed, thrive, and blossom? Some of the attributes displayed by individuals with high soul energy are empathy, kindness, generosity, patience, discipline, positivity, love, and much more. At a depleted level, is it any wonder that such empowering attributes are at an all-time low? Your ability to withstand shocks and not react to any and every input is directly connected to your soul energy levels. If your soul is energy-depleted, can you expect a display of empathy, kindness, generosity, and patience? Your ability to withstand shocks and control your reactions is the quality of a high energy soul. I ask you, if your soul energy was low, would you have the power to remain non-reactive?

In 2023, I conducted a poll on LinkedIn where I asked people to share their main reasons for anxiety. The options given were as follows:

- Work-related stress
- Financial constraints
- Feeling out of control
- Too many burdens

I could have never predicted the results. They are given below:

- Too many burdens - 30%
- Work-related stress - 26%
- Financial constraints - 23%
- Feeling out of control - 21%

Struggling with financial constraints or a stressful job can be easily quantified. However, feeling burdened is not a tangible or quantifiable measure but an emotion. It highlights the depletion of energy at the level of the soul. Just as hunger and prolonged fasting can weaken the physical body by not allowing it to function at peak capacity, a weakened soul cannot connect to happiness or the positivity within. A soul with depleted energy reduces its capacity for growth. The feeling of burden is the direct result of this decreased capacity.

It is said that happiness is generated from within. If you are responsible for your happiness, where is it currently? Why are you not feeling happy and why does life feel like a burden? For nearly 1/3rd of those who responded to my poll, its impact was more potent than work-related stress and financial constraints.

You are all aware of Intelligence Quotient (IQ) and Emotional Quotient (EQ). However, you have certainly forgotten the Happiness Quotient (HQ). This book is my answer to all those who seek their HQ and want to energise their soul power, to be so replete with energy that the Ferrari of your life doesn't stall and sputter due to lack of fuel but cruises at top speed.

The tools and techniques shared here create healing and self-awareness and enhance HQ. They have been instrumental in my evolvement. It is my sincere wish that every one of you must also achieve this heightened sense of peace, happiness, bliss, and transcendent joy.

Part 1

CHAPTER

01

What Changed Outside

The world as you know it has changed. You are no longer living in the same world as your parents and definitely not that of your grandparents. There has been a major shift in between these worlds. This shift is not just related to what you eat, what you wear or what you think. The change is deeper and can be viewed in all the elements around us.

I challenge you to watch the movies that your grandparents liked. Your fingers will automatically itch to reach for the remote to replace the earlier slow-paced movies with something slick and fast-paced. My generation grew up watching old movies and developed a deep appreciation for them. I find that my son's generation has evolved beyond this. You can view the landing page of any OTT provider to see that movies centred around crime are in the blockbuster and most viewed list.

I too appreciate this change. My own viewing preferences have changed too. The world has become fast paced. The old black-and-white Hindi movies had a lot of dialogue, and the progress was slow along with way too many songs.

A classic example of this difference was seen during a family party. Someone mentioned Raj Kapoor. My son glanced my way and innocently enquired, "Who is Raj Kapoor?"

For any Indian of my generation, this question is blasphemous. I mean, he was a great showman and had made some amazing movies, leaving behind a legacy of movies that I had loved while growing up. But these are boring for my son. He loves all the Fast and the Furious ones (pun intended) where the characters swiftly move through a series of events that always keep you on the edge of your seat. There is an OMG (Oh my God!) moment every 5 to 10 minutes.

It's no wonder that the movies of an earlier era seem so slow to my son and others of his generation and consequently 'oh so boring.' To keep up with the hunger for more exciting and dopamine-raising content, filmmakers, news channels, and entertainment providers have quickened the pace of films. What was 16 frames per second in the era of silent films is now fast-paced with digital filming techniques. Does this make a big difference? It may create a difference in one area of our lives but is this effect confined to just that area?

When seen as a whole, the overall effect of this change in viewing preferences on you is phenomenal and life-changing. You have been slowly conditioned to increase your reaction levels as you look for excitement in all areas of your life. This increase in pace also majorly accounts for the decrease in concentration levels you are witnessing nowadays.

Anyone with kids can definitely relate to this. All kids at some point have come up to their parents and said the three dreaded words, "I am bored."

It's a constant struggle to keep your child engaged. What is different between kids and adults? Mainly their perception of time.

How does time change?

Activity

Start your stopwatch, close your eyes, and count up to 60 seconds. Open your eyes when you feel a minute might have passed. Check whether you were right and compare the minute that you perceived with your eyes closed with the actual stopwatch. The result can be any of the options given below:

1. Your mental minute was slower than that of the stopwatch
2. Your mental minute was in the same range as that of the stopwatch
3. Your mental minute was faster than that of the stopwatch

If you are older, your mental minute will definitely be slower. A child's mental minute would be much faster.

So which one is it?

If your mental minute is faster, you are not alone. You are definitely a part of the growing number of adults who are experiencing and are immersed in this **faster** time universe. You are used to 4G and now 5G technology.

The digital age

For me, the start of the digital age was not the advent of computers. The early computers were just meant to compute or calculate. My introduction to this amazing new world took place during my college days. I had enrolled for a fashion design diploma at SNDT University in Juhu, Mumbai, in 1990. We received guidance on using the CAD (Computer Aided Designing) software on the computer to draw sketches, namely a croquis. This is the rough sketch figure that all designers use while fleshing out their creations. These were the days before the stylus, the trackball, and the mouse, which we use so confidently nowadays, were invented. We used the up, down, and side-to-side arrows on the keyboard to create our croquis. Believe me, it was a painstaking and extremely frustrating process, especially if you made even a slight mistake. Correcting the mistake was more time-consuming, and like everyone, I too hailed the invention of the trackball. This provided much-needed relief. Along with everyone, I too welcomed all the advances and inventions related to technology with open arms. Those were exciting times. I especially love the way technology is being used now, leading to the digitalisation of everything to make life simple.

However, what changes did this upgrade in technology bring to other areas of your life? Once things were made simple, it translated into a hunger for more. You can see this effect all around you. As a species, the homo sapiens faced this quantum leap without realising the effect it would have on mental and emotional well-being. For instance, from being patient and accepting people who waited for the crops to grow, farmers have evolved into hunters who are always on the prowl for more. What is next? I want more. Where is the next big thing? I want… I want more. I want NOW.

Does this resonate with you? Can you see it happening around you? It has become so much a part of what you are as humans. It's not just limited to technological advances but the way you devour content. You are constantly on the lookout for more. You take only a split second to see a video on YouTube and immediately switch to another one.

The analytics team behind every application and social media platform is constantly evaluating and analysing which content is working well and which isn't. Some things they look at include what are the demographics of the viewership and what is the bounce rate.

These aspects were eye-openers for me. In 2019, I started writing a blog and created my blog page under www.vriin.com. Though it was meant to be just a platform to express myself, it started evolving based on the feedback I received. I learnt about SEO (Search Engine Optimisation) as it seemed my content was not reaching the right audience. There is an overload of suggestions on how you can maximise your content.

The best parameter is the bounce rate. It tells you how many visitors clicked on your page and closed it within a second. The lesser the bounce rate, the better your content. The activity that I had started as a means of just sharing my thoughts became a monumental task of looking at SEO recommendations and keeping track of bounce rates. This slowly escalated into a gargantuan task and seemed to take over my life. More than writing content that I liked, I was focused on SEO and what I could change. I realised my writing was not based on what would provide value to others but on what would please them. After 6 months of posting my blogs, I chose to take a break from this constant cycle. This break incidentally coincided with the advent of the Covid pandemic (March 2020).

Covid brought on a period of reflection not just for me but for the entire world. You could see that it made the biggest leap in everyone's working style. The line between work and home started vanishing. Companies could now access all their employees 24 x 7 via their mobile at any time and anywhere. Laptops replaced the staid location-specific desktop computers. What was the initial reaction? Relief. Yes, jobs were safe. Work was getting done. It was a giant leap forward for technology. As a Human Resources (HR) professional, you could say that I was in the thick of the entire workplace transformation.

There had been a quantum leap earlier as well in the decade from 2000 to 2010. I remember the excitement when I started using my first Blackberry—the qwerty keypad, the Blackberry Messenger, and the trackpad that worked just like a mini mouse. It started a trend. I was no longer required to access my desktop computer and could access my emails wherever and whenever I desired. Technology is supposed to make our lives easier. Yes, it did. But are you using it to make your lives easier or are you complicating matters further?

What was the biggest result of these shifts? There was absolutely no downtime. What was earlier exciting had now become commonplace. This merging of your work and personal lives became seamless. Don't start taking cudgels against me and defending technology. The intention behind these inventions is amazing and the invention itself is not at fault. The fault is in the way you use it. What started as a convenience has now completely taken over your life.

What did the technological advances change? You are no longer living in your parents' era when there was a clear demarcation in the time allotted to work, family, hobbies, friends, community, prayers, and much more. There was a time when work ended (at the end of the working day) and restarted the next day morning with downtime in between.

Some of you might remember 'The Great Resignation' in 2021 that followed Covid. The chance to spend time at home with the family was the start of a transformation of sorts. People realised that they could not live their lives like robots and could choose a life of quality over the race to do and achieve more while prioritising wealth creation. This was a short-lived phenomenon and many chose to return to their steady jobs. But Covid was the biggest nudge that society took towards evolvement. There was a spark of a movement that differentiated between what is acceptable and what is not. While working hours got better in some companies with an improvement in work culture as the focus, a majority of them chose to follow the same routine, forgetting that Covid had knocked on their doors and tried to leave an important message.

CHAPTER 02

The Start of the Change

We are not makers of history. We are made by history

– Martin Luther King Jr.

Giani Sant Singh Ji Maskeen, a great Sikh philosopher and *kathavachak* (giver of discourses) once said that mankind will stop evolving if it forgets its history. You will then keep repeating the mistakes of your predecessors. I remember thinking that there was an actual purpose to history and it was not just something that you are compelled to learn in school.

If history is the building block of present-day scenarios, you can actually trace how society has changed. The world witnessed a lot of change in the 20th century, more than ever before. This century watched the Industrial and Technological Revolutions take place. It saw two World Wars, other location-specific wars, and countless other conflicts, struggles, agitations and movements. This century also bore witness to the birth of feminism, freedom of expression, an awareness of racism, and the first steps towards its eradication. Cultural borders started shrinking through globalisation. There was a re-emergence of the spiritual and self-healing movements. There were many great thinkers, philosophers, preachers, and healers who kickstarted this process. You, as a part of this new world, are reaping the benefits.

The contribution of Martin Luther King Jr., Rosa Parks and many others was the start of the awareness movement for racial equality. The suffragette movement in England started off the feminist and equal rights movement for women.

When I think of World War II, the Holocaust and its horrors come to mind. When I first read the book by Viktor E. Frankl on 'Man's Search for Meaning,' my immediate reaction was, "Yes, we are aware of the effect the mind has on our thinking and its effect on our circumstances."

I have read these works and have been inspired by many other philosophers, healers and spiritual beings like Louise Hay, Diana Cooper, James Redfield, Rhonda Byrne and many others. I became aware of the important part the mind plays in all that we achieve. Other writers have spoken about the mind and its effect on our reality earlier like Swami Vivekananda, Paramhansa Yogananda, William Walker Atkinson, James Allen, George Gurdjieff and many others. However, I believe that the world started taking note only after the mid-twentieth century. It was a revelation to read the book 'Man's Search For Meaning' by Viktor E. Frankl. He was a psychologist who went through the horrendous, debilitating, and mind-numbing experience of World War II. His words take on new meaning when reviewed in light of what really happened to him and countless others. His personal life-changing experiences credence to the knowledge shared by others and added to the existing equation.

India too was struggling when these events were happening across the world. The country had been freed from colonial rule in 1947 but faced the tragedy of the Partition (the great divide). It had been stripped of its riches and had a long history of invasions and occupations. In the past, India had been known for her culture, spirituality and courageous leaders. We had the Maurya Dynasty, the Chola Dynasty, King Asoka, the Buddha, and Lord Mahavir. India remains the land of the Ramayana, the Bhagwad Gita, and the Vedas and all its teachings. This proud history was obscured by all that happened later. It is only now that a revival of sorts is happening with changes taking place. However, we can also observe the duality not just in India but also in the world. On one hand, there are countless spiritual beings, gurus, healers, and philosophers. On the other, India has an equally strong presence of corruption, hate, strife, conflicts, displacements, struggles, and so much more.

What brought on this duality? Where did the society go wrong? What could have been done differently? Could this have been managed better?

To understand this, it's important to understand history. History is the pillar on which the tower of awakening is built. Without knowing the cause of all the strife, we cannot effect change. A surgeon cannot patch up a wound without knowing what caused it in the first place. Knowing the cause, learning the why and accepting the why will make us aware and only then can lasting and universal change take place.

Like the rest of the world, India too was torn apart by wars, within the country as well as outside its borders. India under colonial rule was a part of World War II. While the world recovered, India continued to struggle for its independence and development.

My intention here is not to delve deeper into the actual events but to bring forth the reason why we are facing this duality. The India of our grandfathers and fathers is vastly different from the one that we grew up in. They grew up in a post-independence, post-partition era in the presence of scarcity and without globalisation. While the world quickly moved on after the two World Wars and focused on continuing the innovations of the Industrial Revolution and later creating the technological revolution, India continued to struggle. She saw further wars with her neighbours and countless other conflicts brought about as a result of the scarcity created by these events. Development took second place to mere survival.

The generation of your grandfathers was a part of this history. The conflict was at their doorstep and they too had to learn how to survive. While the conflicts were taking place across India, North India bore the brunt of the attacks more severely compared to South India. You will still find many ancient temples and cultural places intact in South India. The northern and eastern parts of India were stripped of many of their places of worship, and their cultural and commercial hubs.

I belong to a North Indian family that was directly affected by the Partition of India in 1947. My maternal and paternal families migrated from what was the western part of Punjab, which is now in Pakistan, to what became modern-day India. Like all others who were affected, they left behind their homes, their lands, their work, and life as they knew it and depended on handouts to survive. Some members of my family were more badly affected than others. Some others were lucky. It is undeniable that although they worked hard, and not just survived but thrived, there was always a part of them that just could not forget their past and the homes and friends that they had left behind. I remember my grandmother often expressing a longing to visit the home she left behind in Saidpur, now in Pakistan.

Across India, people were recovering and rebuilding their lives, their pride, and their reason for being. However, a scarcity mindset had set in. From being satisfied and contented with their lot, their mindset shifted towards survival and providing a good life for their children. Children who grew up in the 50s and 60s saw their parents struggle for survival. This created a generation of people who changed their focus from spirituality and contentment to the acquisition of money and power.

Believe me, I am not condoning the desire to acquire wealth and power. In essence, it is not a bad thing. Desiring abundance in your life is good and will be covered later in the book. How can you have everything? Abundance, contentment, peace, bliss, and much more.

However, the greed to acquire money at any cost creates strife. It is wrong to want money not for what it can provide but as a means to create power. The action of acquiring money for its sake and to gain power comes with consequences. People want money so that it can be hoarded and used to create power. There is no end to this want, wanting at any cost, and to acquire money via *saam, daam, dand, bhed.* This is an Indian saying that talks about acquiring something by hook or by crook, that is, even by using legal or illegal means.

- Saam - Flattery
- Daam - Paying any price
- Dand - Punishment, torture
- Bhed - Divide and conquer

From working hard to provide a comfortable living for their family, the next generation of Indians focused on lifestyle. From the 1970s onwards everyone shifted to the 'I want more' bandwagon. This was the era where the world was destroyed extensively. There was an uncaring attitude towards planet Earth. Forests were felled to make way for more land. Development was placed above everything else. The environment was neglected and the rights of other species were ignored to satisfy the greed of hungry and selfish humans. What the world saw as progress was at the cost of everything else.

The world was viewed in black and white. You were either rich or nothing. I remember an advertisement tagline 'Yeh Dil Maange More' (the heart wants more). This sums up the corruption and acquisition of power that the world witnessed from the 70s onwards. Becoming rich was the new bandwagon everyone wanted to jump on. Girls wanted rich husbands. Boys wanted rich wives. Everyone wanted to acquire this wealth at the cost of everything else. Dil

Maange More. More and More. Everyone wanted a slice of the good life at all costs by *saam, daam, dand,* and *bhed.*

This change was visible not only in India but was taking place around the world. You can connect the dots. Every service provider applied this element to their marketing strategy. Schools and colleges promoted their ability to get you a high-paying job. Personal ethics were compromised and money became the new God. Politicians around the world became power-hungry and the world of corruption took on a new meaning. The amount of power-grabbing, focus on riches at all costs, and defrauding others for personal gain were things that gained momentum during the latter half of the 20th century. This was unprecedented and unheard of earlier.

There had been instances of kings, emperors, conquerors, dictators, and landlords who had gone all out but now it was a free for all. Everyone wanted in. Multi-level marketing schemes were launched. Fraudsters and tricksters increased. Everything was touted as the next big thing and you were promised a piece of the pie and an entry into the world of the uber rich at any cost.

Corporations grew and promised everyone a brighter future while corporate life started attracting all and sundry. Everyone wanted to be associated with the bigger and better brands as association with something bigger was seen as the route to an abundant life.

As you do anything, so will you do everything

- Martha Beck.

This one-track focus on hunting and grabbing a larger share of the proverbial money pie created a generation of individuals who compromised their integrity, the safety of their fellow humans, and much more.

There is a line in the Guru Granth Sahib that says that there will come a time when women will become personified as objects and men will become hunters. Does this seem familiar? I remember watching comedy series like the **Benny Hill show, Are You Being Served, Allo Allo,** and **MASH** in the '80s and '90s and finding them hilarious. However, now when I view them through a new lens, they upset me as the women in those shows were objectified and characterised as sluts. This was a free-for-all that was considered normal. It was this attitude of hunting without any resistance that saw the rise of all the predators in the world like the Howard Weinsteins and Jeffery Epsteins. Their names are here just because of the media magnifying them but you and I are both aware that they are not the only ones.

You can all relate to the people in your lives who have tried to hunt and compromise your ideals while showing you a glimpse of the big life. I had hoped that after the momentous, path-breaking, and empowering #MeToo movement, there would be no more instances of casting couch or office predators who promised largesse in return for benefits. But I doubt that. As long as you as a society are shown that money is the ONLY yardstick for success, some individuals may be prepared to compromise their integrity for an easy route.

If you refer to most news channels and society magazines, their definition of success is clear. You only need to type rich people in the search engine for the list of richest people in the world, in each country. Their net worth is given next to their names.

Movies that have done business of 100 crores in India are said to be hits while the others are flops. This message is constantly bombarded at us from all corners and has made people compromise their values. What started as something temporary and as a means of survival, became ingrained within you and you started believing that this was the only way.

I repeat, being rich is not bad. All the good in the world is actually done through wealth. Wealth is the fuel that creates change. It however needs to be wealth with values and not just wealth for wealth's sake. Instead of mentioning the net worth next to each name, can the list of richest people reflect the change brought forth by each individual?

The mentality of the hunter that was applied to the acquisition of wealth was applied to all areas of life. The hunter-like quality created individuals who are unsatisfied with their lot in life. For such individuals, food needed to be more exciting. Staid, old, boring home-cooked and healthy food was replaced with fast food which was greasy and your diet was overdosed with sweetened, calorie-rich food choices.

As the single-minded pursuit of money grew, so did the fear. The fear of losing it, once again being weak or dependent on others, to go through the scarcity that personified the lives of your parents. Ironically, this scarcity was not felt so acutely by the previous generation who actually went through the worst years. This was the generation of your grandfathers. All they felt was an immense gratitude for what they had. The next generation, of your fathers, that grew up after these turbulent times became immersed in the scarcity mindset. It is majorly your childhood experiences that define your mindset. Children growing up in an environment of love, respect, patience, and acceptance will automatically be more emotionally stable as compared to those who lacked these essential qualities during their formative years.

The children who grew up lacking these qualities, in turn, created a further vacuum in their children. The gap between what you were and what you have become started widening. It was this lack that created an escapist mindset. Everyone has created their escape route by escaping while being in plain sight. You might be talking to someone who is playing a mobile game. Family members sitting together are more engaged online rather than finding common ground offline. Spending time around older members of the family, who are slow and boring is replaced with spending time on mobiles and in a digital and fast-moving arena.

Visual social media viewing that was earlier laid back has now moved to hunched forward. By laid back I mean you used to watch content on television while seated in a comfortable position or while lying back. This was replaced with being hunched forward while viewing content that is short, in the form of reels since you want to be entertained quickly.

The number of gaming apps, game stations, and fast-moving content available today is phenomenal and at never-seen-before levels.

As an HR professional, my team has conducted one or two-day training programmes but this has given way to capsule learning and even gamification. Yes, gamification has been there for some time now. Games are created around the learning topic and each correct answer gives you a score. Instant gratification has created a hyper, overstimulated and constantly on-the-go brain. This attitude of escapism has created several avenues.

Internal journeys involving good old-fashioned soul searching have been replaced with external gratification. The habit of reading books for entertainment and learning has been sacrificed and replaced with binge-watching series and surfing online channels for constant content. This creates a constant need for more and more hunting.

This has given rise to a plethora of feelings: not satisfied with the content (rooted in escapism), seeking more and more content, not taking the time to sit back and absorb it but making split-second decisions, and clicking on it once and labelling it as boring a second later. Do you remember the bounce rate? The bounce rate does not capture the value of the content but the extent of the individual's escapism. Instead of analysing content, it is the individual who needs to be analysed.

Is this related to increasing emotional, mental, and physical health issues? What do you think?

India vs other countries

This phenomenon of escapism, wanting more, and constantly hunting is common across the world. You have truly achieved globalisation. With regard to work culture, India has always been playing its own game. The events of the last century and the associated scarcity and upheaval created a generation that was embedded with the fear of losing money. The need for security and assurance was scored higher than consciousness and self-respect. Jobs in India are associated with self-worth. You may have heard of other countries where getting the pink slip is common. There is no shame attached to losing your job. This is not the case in India—at least among the generation who grew up in the last century. The millennials are redefining their work culture with their ability to take risks and start new ventures. They want more freedom but the earlier generation is still seeking the security of a prestigious job. How can you test this? Just ask your father if you can quit your job in a prestigious company to start a business. How do you think he will react? I know that my mother was horrified when I quit my job. I know several others who had the same reaction.

This has certainly been exploited by the companies. While the world is moving from a five to a four-day week, in India, for the most part, we are still working five or six days a week. There is no boundary between work and personal life. I read about Germany where 8 pm is considered late. Managers are discouraged from calling their team after 8 pm. This is not the case in India. In the corporate sector, calling your team at all hours is a common occurrence. This may be sometimes even as late as midnight. The more senior you are, the worse it gets. Weekends too are not your own. Working late is considered prestigious and you get recognised for your hard work and so-called diligence.

With the advent of laptops, mobiles and online meetings, the boundary of time has been eradicated. Everyone is constantly on call. This has actually gotten worse with Covid. Now managers have realised that the same productivity can be expected even when the employee is working from home. Meetings are arranged online and even employees who are on leave are expected to join.

Maybe not all companies in India are following this but the overall work culture encourages sitting late and over-extending. An ex-colleague of mine had his WhatsApp status set to 'Hard work is rewarded with more hard work.' This is so true.

The root of this blind acceptance of a toxic work culture lies in fear. More specifically, the fear of losing the job and the fear of a return to the era of scarcity. Indians around the world aim for education, not just to expand their mind but to get good jobs. The learning is aimed only at acquiring a prestigious job and accepting the toxic work culture as their job defines who they are.

The rat race is well and truly active.

Social prestige

One can become great by association. I was once associated with a stock broking and wealth management company as an HR professional. We were required to often visit the Head Office for Group HR meetings. We would travel to the fancy headquarters in a prestigious South Mumbai (Nariman Point) address. I recall that there were six lifts (elevators) to travel up to your floor with one lift reserved for Directors. Once when travelling with the head of my department, who was a Director herself, we entered the lift designated for directors. The liftman insolently stated that only directors were allowed, making it clear that we were not welcome. My companion calmly stared him down and informed him that she too was a director. During the entire journey, he kept staring at us and seemed clearly upset.

Later the head of my department shared a piece of wisdom, something she was famous for. She remarked, "How strange that some men become big just by association."

The lift operator was clearly considered the top dog among the men operating the lifts because he manned the one reserved for directors.

This is the prestige our jobs give us. Like the liftman, you too may be guilty of associating your self-worth with your job. We adjust and adapt our self-respect and consciousness to continue our association only with companies that have a brand value. Everyone wants to work for big brands and wants to gain prestige by association. It is good to work with such giants as they are market leaders after all. But it cannot be without a sense of self and at the cost of your integrity and self-respect. There is immediate validation though it may be at the cost of personal sacrifice. Acceptance of corruption and power play is more rampant at senior levels in big corporations rather than at junior levels. Everyone wants to get onto this bandwagon. The reasons remain the same: fear of scarcity, and the fear of losing money and prestige by association. However, Covid made people realise how precarious life is and resulted in the Great Resignation.

Many companies have then started changing their work culture and I hope this trend continues.

I remember hearing about this gentleman who retired from a top government position in Mumbai. He felt completely isolated post-retirement as during his tenure, he had not taken the time to cultivate any friendships. The prestige of his job had sustained him throughout his career and without that important and exceptional umbrella, he was lost. No job, no matter how prestigious, should be associated with your self-worth. Self-worth comes from within and should be able to stand alone.

While the events of the last century changed the way people behaved, these were all external changes. For change to happen, you need to examine what is happening internally. The rise in suicides, road rage, mental health issues, and emotional isolation is a reflection of the increased pressures being faced by everyone. Being aware of the how, the where, the what, and the when is the diagnostic tool. For healing to begin, the pressure within you has to be diagnosed correctly. Be aware of the areas of your life where pressure has been building up steadily. The image that you are required to project to the world is different from your inner self. Self-awareness leads to self-mastery and transformation. Your self-mastery will slowly release the pressure within and you can start the process of self-healing.

Part 2

What Changed Inside

How does the past shape you?

All incidents from your past are building blocks that have either created walls (blockages) or doorways (openings) in your life. The walls are the negative beliefs that you have absorbed and the doorways are the positive reinforcements that make you more accepting of change as compared to others around you.

You may recall the story of baby elephants being conditioned to accept shackles on their feet, shackles that they could have easily broken as adults. However, their conditioning defines their future, whether they see a doorway or just a brick wall. The same can be said for everyone. The conditioning and beliefs that have been around you from early childhood have created blocks or areas of comfort that you don't want to be parted from.

I grew up in a conservative, patriarchal North Indian family based in Mumbai, then Bombay, with walls all around me. Who has seen the Hindi movie 'Dilwale Dulhaniya Le Jayenge' starring Shahrukh Khan, Kajol, and Amrish Puri? There is a scene at the beginning of the movie where the mother (played by Farida Jalal) and her two daughters are dancing, laughing, and plainly enjoying themselves when they realise that the father (played by actor Amrish Puri) is expected home. They immediately transform into the perfect, docile, obedient, dutiful, and pious family, and this sets the trend for the entire movie. I could relate to this movie as it showcased my life with my father playing the role immortalised by Amrish Puri.

My mother, my sister and I grew up with all sorts of rules, regulations, and well-meant boundaries. We were to wake up by 7 am. In the event we were sleepy, we could have our bath, make our bed and then go back to sleep. Who does that? Seriously? There were many such absolute laws in my family that I accepted blindly.

No matter where we were, we had to return home latest by 7:30 pm, before my father came home from his office. This was an absolute rule and I can recall one harrowing instance, during my college days, when I had to travel to Churchgate for some research. I got delayed and panicked when I realised that I was on the same train as my father. The inherent fear of getting delayed and reaching home after my father made me hide at the bus stop near Bandra station. While my father took bus number 214, which had a stop close to our home, I dashed to catch bus number 211 which stopped further away. I remember pleading with the driver to stop the bus between two stops just to reach home earlier. Ignoring the danger, I actually disembarked from the bus while it was still moving, ran across the street to my home and rushed into my grandmother's room to hide my bag. My grandmother quickly understood and was very supportive. Maybe she too was a bit scared of my father.

Our fear of returning later than 7:30 pm remained even after my father died in 2014. For a few years post that, my mother would still get palpitations at 7 pm and would say, "It's late. We need to return home." This became my mission and I would deliberately plan outings, intentionally delaying my mother so that she would reach home after 7:30 pm. It took some years but, finally, my mother overcame her panic related to it.

I'm sure you too have had similar experiences, maybe not exactly like mine but similar invisible walls that start defining you. The beliefs of your parents and surroundings guide you into alleys and labyrinths that you would not have taken normally. All our **isms**, like racism, chauvinism, feminism, etc. seemed to have originated somewhere in this space.

I tried with the best of intentions and to the best of my ability that my son would not grow up with these debilitating beliefs and conditioning. However, I later realised that my attempt to free up my life and encourage him to make his own decisions was also an unconscious conditioning from my side. There will always be situations where you could have done better, where you could have guided your children better. As parents, you will always make mistakes and not behave like the parent your child desires. You may have the best of intentions but you can keep trying. I have a ready and crazy sense of humour, and I tend to laugh at the silliest and least funny things.

When he was 21, my son once cheekily reprimanded me, "You have ruined my life."

"Ruined? How?" I asked him.

"You laugh at all my jokes. I thought I was funny. Turns out, I'm not," he clarified. Wasn't that funny? And also a great learning.

I realised then that no matter what you do as parents, you will still create invisible walls around your children and hence it is important for you to also forgive your parents. While this looks good in theory, it took me many years and a lot of forgiving to overcome my unconscious conditioning. I spent years creating doorways and tunnels through the thick walls that had caged me in. I hope my child has fewer walls to break and finds more doorways open than I did.

As an English Literature student, I came across the poem 'My Last Duchess' by Robert Browning, published in 1842. We had lively discussions about this poem in class and what I remember was the Duke showing the painting of his last Duchess to someone. What the Duke is not aware of is how his careful words are creating a word picture and showing him in a bad light.

It is the same with each one of you.

All the events of the past century and the events you have experienced have shaped you into the individuals you are today. They are your windows to the outside world. You may try to hide your inner core but your behaviours, reactions and words will reveal you to the outside world. All of you wear masks, hiding your innermost beliefs but the effect of your past shapes how you think, act, and react no matter how hard you try to hide.

You can do an activity here. Write down your five favourite animals. Now next to each animal, write down what you like about these animals. Don't be content with writing only one or two qualities, dig deeper. Write down at least five to six qualities that you associate with that particular animal. Now review the qualities that you have jotted down. The qualities valued by you will give you a glimpse into your soul.

I recall someone I was coaching mentioned liking dogs. The quality she most admired was the dog's ability to not hold any grudges. Dogs always show their love even though you might have accidentally hurt them. Someone else valued dogs because of their adventurous spirit. You can guess from these responses about who is carrying the burden of hurt within themselves.

A client of mine mentioned loving turtles. The ability of the turtle to retreat into their shell in times of danger. He had approached me to overcome the trauma of his father's death and find peace within. When questioned further about what events in his past made him want a safe place, he was shocked. He later revealed it was his father's explosive nature and the fights he had witnessed while growing up. It is no wonder that the turtle was a favourite animal for him. As he overcame the trauma, his favourite animals and the reasons for his liking also changed.

The transformation starts creating a new you. Another of my mentees called this his 2.0 version and added that with newer updates better versions of him are getting created. Wouldn't you love to have a newer and updated version of you? I loved this analogy, didn't you?

How does the past shape your soul?

Your soul is pure bliss and happiness. It is unadulterated joy and divine.

Imagine you have a room in your home that is full of all the riches you desire. There are mountains of gold, silver, and diamonds. The room itself is shining because of its abundance. It's like a glowing bulb with infinite voltage. Your access to this room is restricted till you have cleared and cleaned all other areas of your home. You normally get so tied up in the other rooms or areas of your home that you actually forget that such a blissful room exists. Forgetting about this room does not mean it doesn't exist. It is present in every one of you. It's normal to focus on the pain in the third toe of your left foot rather than realising that the rest of your body is healthy. This is a human tendency. It's normal.

During a recent discussion, someone mentioned that the soul is pure and does not change. Yes, the soul is unchanging and pure. Just like a baby. A baby is born with a pure heart. You just have to hear a baby laughing to feel the divinity of its soul. Are you like that? Do you still laugh with that same abandon? Can you still feel that bliss that makes the baby in you gurgle and chuckle with innocence? What has changed?

While I graduated with English Literature as my major, I took psychology as my minor. During one of our memorable sessions, the discussion centred around man and society and two opposite fields of thought —man is born pure; society corrupts him vs. man is born wild; society civilises him. While the first quote can be associated with Jean-Jacques

Rousseau (Man is born free but is everywhere in chains), I don't know the origin of the second one. While I can't now go back and get more clarity, both these sayings left a deep impression in my mind. Both are correct but so diverse. So, which one is true?

It's the same with your soul. Your soul is born free, pure, happy, blissful, and simply full of joy. It is the layers that you have since added over this that are now clouding your mind. Imagine that the sun is shining outside your window in all its glory but you have secluded yourself in a room with thick drapes drawn over opaque, dark, and dusty windows. The soul is pure but all the layers covering it have dulled its happiness.

The poll mentioned earlier showed that many of you are still living with burdens. What has created these burdens? Is it the society around you? Are you feeling the weight of the burdens that society has imposed upon you? What are the layers that have been added to your soul preventing you from seeing the sunlight?

You can compare these layers to an onion. Several such layers are hiding the core. To uncover the core and access the pure bliss within, the layers need to be peeled back one at a time. This is not the time to use a sharp knife and slice through them. These sharp knives and the wounds received during your lifetime have created these layers in the first place. Can you remember what it felt like when someone at your workplace, from your family or friends, said something cutting? It felt like a piece of you had been sliced away. You immediately felt a quickening of your heart, a sinking sensation, and a lessening of your energy. These are instances when you are not only getting cut but are actually adding one more layer of safety to your already bruised and battered heart. Your emotions are meant for your comfort but are always trying to keep you safe.

Activity

When you think of the following emotions, what are the thoughts that come to mind?

- Trust -
- Fear -
- Confusion -
- Anger -
- Irritation -
- Guilt -
- Disgust -
- Embarrassment -

- Anxiety -
- Shame -
- Jealousy -

When you think of certain members of your family, friends, colleagues, associates or anyone else in your community, do you feel any of the above emotions? Can you identify who makes you feel them? When do one or more of these emotions swirl up? You will probably realise that the same sensations actually helped form the layer in the first place. There is an immediate shift in reality and you are no longer functioning from a place of optimism and trust but have changed your clear vision to dusty and opaque spectacles.

This journey to delve deeper within your consciousness is a process that will free you and make you feel empowered. Your awareness will enable you to express yourself.

I remember reading an article on LinkedIn entitled 'The Deer and the Lion' written by Rahul Jain from Brain & Co. The full post can be accessed at https://www.linkedin.com/pulse/deer-lion-rahul-jain/. I will talk about it here briefly.

A deer is peacefully grazing on a grassland when she realises she is being stalked by a lion. She immediately springs into action and runs for her life. Her timely action saves her life. Once she realises the danger has passed, she resumes grazing and is peaceful.

Now imagine the same scenario if the deer had human-like emotions. The deer is now probably scarred for life thinking that she would be attacked from behind. She could be open to attack by all predators. She cannot trust herself to go about alone and needs people around to keep her safe. She feels that the entire world is full of big bad lions. She will probably never approach the meadow without the resurgence of the same emotions she felt at the time of the initial attack. While the danger has passed for the deer, the emotions that surfaced during the event are still very much a part of her life and have created another layer around her soul. Another pair of spectacles through which she views the world. In humans, this becomes another layer of protection, a proverbial band-aid added to your layered soul.

What this has also created is a reaction. A reaction that is associated with one or more emotions. In this case, fear is soon followed by distrust, confusion, and even anger. You feel like a victim and probably blame all lions or predators for your state. You go from an empowered and peaceful space to blaming others. You feel like a victim and feel a lack of control. What made sense during the initial flight or fight response stops being relevant after the event. However, the emotions are still swirling around you and all subsequent encounters are affected by this one incident.

Someone I know is in an unhappy marriage. How do I know this? Because in every discussion and conversation, this topic invariably crops up. She freely chooses her words to explain her situation and blames her *kismet* (destiny) for making her endure such trials. While I do agree that she has borne a lot in her life, is it still relevant? She is in her 70s now and is constantly referring to events that transpired during her teens or her 20s and 30s. She does not refer to current events and is still stuck in a loop that ended more than 30 years ago. Her every thought, action and interaction with others is coloured by this never-ending loop that poisons all her relationships.

Why am I mentioning her? Because I found the way you form associations and divisions interesting. These associations were initially based on reality. However, these have now been superseded by other emotions. The original circumstances are no longer relevant but the emotions that were relevant in the past are still colouring her present and consequently her future. She will never believe she is contented as she still views the world through the same 40-year-old lens. She is living in a time warp with all her thoughts and actions being forever coloured by the events of her youth through all the layers her soul has acquired trying to keep her safe. What was a protective shield earlier has now festered since it was left unresolved.

Yes, my acquaintance had an extremely trying time in her 20s and 30s. Her entire perception of reality is rooted in that trying time and her enemies and friends have been defined on that basis and there is no changing that. It seems like an earthquake took place and broke down her home. Though it has been rebuilt, she is still roaming among its ruins. Her brothers have been her strongest supporters. They realised that she had been wronged and provided her with a lot of love, understanding and monetary help. Recognising them as friends, allies, and her only support system, she unconsciously aligned herself with their belief systems to the exclusion of everything else. Challenges that affected her brothers in their business, their political affiliations, and their opinions became the core of her life. She even backed their extreme beliefs, if needed.

Her brothers are successful businessmen and have faced numerous challenges. But they have moved on and she is still living in the same space. At the start of my coaching career, in my innocence and zeal to help, I tried to make her realise the loop that she was stuck in. I realised soon that that loop was her saviour and her safety net. She had a weak soul and derived all her energy from the zeal and fervour that she surrounded herself with. A depleted soul can make you stay in such a loop and stop your progress.

Depleted souls are always the ones getting caught up in others' causes. They want to be associated with a cult, gang or community that cements their perceived sense of reality. Like the operator in the director's lift, they need that heightened sense of self from the things they are associated with and derive their power from them. They do not have an independent sense of identity. To motivate someone to move out from a toxic relationship, you first need to energise their soul. A lack of soul energy will only make them replace one toxic relationship with another or return to their earlier circumstances even after they are provided all the help to start a new life.

Encouraging them to make the right choices and go beyond their current circumstances cannot involve a quick decision and will not be an expeditious process. Their life experiences have created their current reality. Each traumatic experience that is hidden within will need to be reviewed through all the protective layers that surround them, exactly like how you unpeel an onion layer by layer. They will not thank you for abruptly removing them from their toxic surroundings if you do not first support them as they raise their soul energy. For change to take place, healing needs to be instituted first. As they raise their soul energy, they will start creating their own wisdom. This inner wisdom creates awakening and healing. You will get more clarity by reading about the Soul Leadership framework and the 3 Cs shared later in the book.

The world around you is interconnected. You do not exist in isolation. You are connected to everything around you via energy. Your soul energy connects you to the radio frequency of the universe around you. Your relationships, your surroundings, and all the events in your life are connected.

In this section of the book, I've tried to highlight what is energy and how it affects the soul. How does lower soul energy affect you and what transpires when these levels increase? This journey that you are taking with me is one that I embarked on many years ago when I tried to make some sense of my own life. I too was affected by the loop my life was stuck in. Since I managed to successfully clear most of my loops, I felt that this process must be shared with everyone. What took me many, many years to overcome may not be the case for all of you. I used to wish that someone had just handed me a comprehensive book that covered the entire process and not just given me the bits and pieces which I had to fit together like a torturous jigsaw puzzle to rebuild my life.

My attempt with this trilogy is to give you these three comprehensive books that will start your evolvement journey and create energised soul leaders who are in charge of their own lives and not burdened by the loops that their life goes into.

What is soul energy?

Soul energy refers to your connectivity with the universe around you.

Imagine a scenario where you have all the gadgets—mobile phone, notepad, laptop, smartwatch—and suddenly there is a blackout. Your WiFi has conked off. You restart the router, check with your internet service provider, and frantically try to connect through the hotspot but nothing activates the WiFi on your devices. Others can use this connectivity but somehow your devices are just not being supported.

All work comes to a standstill. You're trying to make sense of your new world. You cannot call an Uber, order food through Zomato or Swiggy, or get your groceries through Amazon Fresh or Blinkit. You cannot access your net banking or your investment portfolio. Similarly, your Netflix and Amazon Prime accounts have stopped working. How can you keep track of the clothes you ordered on Amazon and Myntra? All efforts on your part to get back on the grid have failed. Doesn't this seem like an apocalyptic scenario?

I grew up in the '70s and the '80s. During the '60s and '70s, the words ESP (extra sensory perception) grew popular and I remember thinking how would this work? How could thought waves traverse time and space? How does an antenna work? Our television had an antenna that was mounted on the terrace along with those belonging to others in the building. You could count the number of televisions in any building by the number of antennae mounted on the terrace. Each antenna was tall, cumbersome, and clumsy-looking with a tendency to get affected by wind, rain or any other natural phenomena. They had to be positioned in a certain direction to get a clear picture and sound in the televisions they were connected to.

There was a high probability that your television would suddenly stop working, and then the entire drama would begin since your antenna probably needed adjustment. This was no easy task and usually required a minimum of two people. While my father and my uncle would ascend the terrace and try to adjust the antenna, pointing it this way or that, my role was to keep the television switched on, poke my head out of the window and inform them when the picture became clear. They would make adjustments and yell, "Is it clear? Is the TV working?" I would yell back with a no or a final yes. Looking back, this is one activity that I definitely do not miss.

If someone had told me that there would come a day when this activity would become superfluous, I would not have believed them. The WiFi connectivity of today has created smart TVs. You are connected without the cumbersome antennae and their adjustments. So what has changed? Connectivity systems. You have tapped into the world of WiFi, and satellite dishes for each TV and cable TV network. This is a whole new dimension compared to the earlier TV antenna. It is a whole new way of being. Imagine a satellite dish that you can tap into and connect to the energy of the universe. Just imagine the change that this can bring into your life. It opens a whole new dimension.

Just like the WiFi connectivity, your soul too is connected to the universe around you through its energy field. Each soul is part of this grid. Your interactions with others are not individual but are part of an entire network. Your perceptions of this grid vary based on your connection to it.

The physics of things

While I was learning physics in school, I considered it a subject that we had to learn and get graded on. It was only later that I realised the majesty of physics. How do different forms of energy interact with each other? For instance, a napkin drying on the clothesline is not a simple process. There is a reaction taking place. The molecules of water present in the napkin are decreasing slowly due to the energy from the sun and this leads to drying.

You are all beings filled with energy. The entire universe is connected with energy and there is a constant give and take of energy taking place. You are all reacting to others around you. There is a constant flow of energy and all our interactions are a result of this energy exchange.

We spoke of the layers created around your soul earlier. The soul energy that is coursing through you and the entire universe flows in relation to these layers. Every experience where you feel unsafe, traumatised, and divided creates more and more layers around you. Now imagine that these layers are creating blocks and the energy that was supposed to flow easily is getting diverted. You are not receiving the complete share of energy that is your right. This does not have to do with the energy grid as it is connected but the energy needs to flow through the multiple layers surrounding you.

You can also compare this to a field of landmines. Each negative experience and layer that was created has contributed to creating another landmine beneath your feet. These are not visible to the naked eye but are very much present. They are unconsciously affecting how you think, how you act and most importantly how you react. The free flow of energy to your soul has become entangled with all these layers and all the landmines that you must avoid.

Imagine if you were asked to roam in this field of landmines. Would you move about freely or would each step be cautious and controlled? Can you associate this concept with your energy field? Due to all these layers, do you think your energy is flowing freely or is it cautious and controlled? If energy flow is limited, how can you really live your life optimally? Remember we discussed Ashish at the end of his 10-day fast. His ability to handle his emotions and troubles is limited as his energy levels are impaired.

Furthermore, as each new layer is added, it changes the chemistry of the existing layers. Or, in other words, adds one more landmine to an already crowded field. This affects the way you perceive the world and also the way the world perceives you. This dictates the life patterns that you have created and are attracting within your lives.

During the Covid pandemic, all of you experienced social isolation. This is however not just related to the pandemic. Your social isolation has been taking place since the last century. From larger, joint families, you have progressed to nuclear families and now to staying alone. The number of people opting to live alone is at an all-time high. The social interaction seen in the previous generations is now unheard of. The world your grandparents lived in consisted of regular community meetings, family gatherings, prayer meets and so much more. With the advent of the digital age and gadgets, we have regressed to a solo state of affairs. Someone intelligently remarked that phones have gotten smarter and people are getting dumber. You have slowly reduced your human interactions which used to be an integral part of energising your soul.

What is the connection between your soul energy and your surroundings?

Energy cannot be studied in isolation. When there is no input, there cannot be a change in the flow of your energy. Your internal layers create a difference in the flow of your energy but what truly harms you is this isolation. Instead of a healthy energy flowing through your reactions, the energy is stagnant and thus debilitating.

The Great Place to Work Employee Engagement Survey places a large premium on camaraderie. It is the pillar of a successful business. The interaction of people (both inter- and intra-department, the ability of everyone to interact, collaborate and form successful teams, and the interpersonal skills involved form the basis of any successful alliance. Any business entrepreneur will vouch for networking. This is the replacement for camaraderie in the business world. The social interaction with other human beings creates camaraderie. Humans need camaraderie in their lives. You have evolved over the years not just because of your intelligence and need for survival but also due to how you have reacted to others within your species.

You can measure this flow of energy through social interactions (compared to social isolation) on a scale of 1 to 10, with 10 being the highest. Measure your inner well-being after 10 days of living alone with no communication with other humans. Note: This is not applicable to saints who are already highly evolved beings but to ordinary mortals like you and me. Now measure your well-being after taking part in events and meetings. Your well-being and ultimately your energy levels will be higher post such social interactions.

Energy begets energy. Your reaction to others creates more energy for you. In a world where you are more engaged with your mobile phones and laptops rather than other people, the energy exchange is restricted. While you are expending your energy, there is no corresponding flow happening from these inanimate sources. This lack of energy input creates more boundaries within you. To really understand how this affects your soul, you need to understand how a soul functions.

What is this universe and how does this energy affect us: The concept of Gami-Verse

Video games available earlier were different. There were separate gaming devices where you could play a particular game. These games were not available at that time in India or they were too expensive. My first video game was purchased in 1986 during my family's first visit to Singapore. I loved that game and spent many hours happily occupied with it.

The first online game that most of my generation played was Snakes. This was the only game that came preinstalled on the Nokia mobile phones and, in my case, the 3315 model. It was fascinating. The tail of the snake kept growing based on the amount of food you kept feeding it and you had to ensure the tail stayed tangle-free throughout its journey.

The primitive games of those times have given way to more evolved and dynamic games that are beautiful to behold, have multiple levels, and have a wealth of details. There are options for multiple players and each player can bring their powers and create their avatars in this dynamic and engrossing Gami-Verse. When playing a game, time just melts away and the cyber universe feels real. Sometimes it seems more realistic than your actual life.

You may have seen the movie 'The Matrix' and marvelled at the unexpected dimension where Neo, Trinity and Morpheus were creating their reality and battling their enemies. They could download different superpowers and learn new skills, upgrading themselves as they moved through the Matrix. I would like you to recollect the start of the movie where Morpheus is instructing Neo on understanding the Matrix. This is a good place to start when you examine how your soul and all the restrictions that you encounter are based on your own limiting beliefs.

It is your own limiting beliefs that stop this flow of energy. While saying this, I earnestly do not recommend that you start jumping off buildings. The Matrix or Gami-Verse as I like to call it is connected to your soul and not your physical body.

How is the Gami-Verse related to your soul?

When do you think of the soul? What is a soul? Is it this pure light that is inside every one of us, telling us to do good? Or do you believe that the soul is this mythical concept that preachers are telling us about? And when it is damned you are definitely going to hell.

Do you imagine hell as this place where it is constantly hot with cauldrons of burning oil? And are you the meat that will be roasting for eternity? All this just because you stole Rs. 10 from your mother's purse when you were 12 and bought a chocolate with it and enjoyed it too. This was the only time I had stolen money and it haunted me for decades. I felt this choice had damned my soul. I spent years trying to overcome this guilt. Or do you believe that you are all pure, powerful souls who are connected with God? If you are all connected, why are so many people suffering? Why did I suffer? Why did I go through depression and emotional abuse? If the soul is so pure, why aren't you all playing harps while seated on clouds? Why don't you laugh the same way now as you did when you were babies? Anyone who has heard a baby laugh can feel the purity of the baby's soul. Why doesn't my laughter still create that magic?

If all souls were equal then everyone should have the same reaction. Identical twins who have every reason for acting in the same way since they have the same DNA are still different people with different reactions. The same event can result in multiple reactions from different people. A team is praised for the multiple inputs and diverse ideas that it can bring. Why is everyone different? Why does someone suffer from road rage and anger issues, whereas someone experiencing the same event will calmly state 'Yes. This happens' and move on?

One of my favourite books during my teens was James Herriot's biography series on his experiences as a vet in rural Yorkshire, England. My mother's school friend Urmila aunty introduced me to a whole new universe of reading when she gifted me this book. The six books were bundled together as an unabridged version and I went through the entire series multiple times. He spoke about the calmness of the Yorkshire farmers who, when confronted with tragedy, would calmly shrug their shoulders and say 'Ay, this happens.' In the preface, I have mentioned a couple of events that took place when I was 20. A marriage had been arranged for me and things were not working out. I wasn't happy and was not able to connect with my fiance. Three weeks before the wedding, my mother decided to speak to my fiance and his parents. My family realised that he was being coerced to marry me and was in love with someone else from a different religion. My mother made a tough call and called off the wedding. This was taboo and unheard of in those days.

As an added pressure, at the time, our family was going through a tough phase financially. To plan another wedding, and make another trousseau for me at this late stage was unthinkable. My mother started getting panic attacks and we could see the tears she was trying to hide. My *nani* (maternal grandmother) was a strong lady. She was deeply religious, supported the community, and someone who gave generously to all religious causes. Many religious leaders, preachers and saints visited my nani's home. My broken engagement coincided with the visit of a saint from

Punjab called Bhai Jasbir Singh Khalsa whom everyone affectionately called Joshi Veerji. Veerji meant brother. Joshi Veerji would regularly visit Mumbai with his many disciples and stay at my nani's home. I remember my mother speaking to him and telling him the entire tale about my broken engagement with tears flowing from her eyes.

He calmly listened to her and gently inquired, "When did this take place?"

She replied, "Two weeks ago."

I still remember this conversation vividly. While I was looking helplessly at my mother, feeling guilty and like a burden and not knowing how I could make her feel better, Joshi Veerji calmly asked, "It's been two weeks and you're still crying?"

My mother looked at him in amazement and I could actually hear her thinking that it had only been two weeks. He gave a gentle and loving explanation and his one line will stay with me till I die.

"When an earthquake occurs, everyone is affected and how quickly you recover depends on the power of your soul (*aatma ki takat*)."

At that moment, my mother, who is a gentle, loving, spiritual and caring person, immediately emerged from her victim mode and healed. My introduction to soul power or the power of the soul was this magical moment. I could immediately associate what he was saying with the Yorkshire farmers so well described by James Herriot. The dots were connected. More understanding did take place over the years but this was my first realisation. No matter what I went through in later years, I knew that when any earthquake affected me, I needed to empower my soul and stand up.

How are your soul, its power and the Gami-Verse connected?

What would you say if you were told that you are all playing your own games? People talk of auras. The outward cloud-like form that surrounds every living thing. Now imagine you are surrounded not just by your aura but by an invisible pod that guides you and shows you only that which you are meant to see. This is an oversimplified way of explaining the Gami-Verse but I request you to bear with me.

What would you say, if you were told that your Gami-Verse can be likened to an invisible pod-like shape that surrounds you wherever you go? Hence you can see others not through your eyes but experience your surroundings through the filters provided by your own Gami-Verse pod. Each experience results in an action or a reaction that creates more levels and more dimensions to your lives. Each game comes with its zones of heaven, hell and everything in between and you keep oscillating between them. You are constantly being made to choose. Choose your path, choose your reactions, choose what tools you require for that portion of the game, and choose whom you would like to team up with. All your choices create more dimensions for you that can either result in an upgrade or the addition of another layer or landmine. Multi-player games bring another dimension to this matrix. Each player plays their own game but somehow contributes to someone else's game as well.

I remember a time when my life was really bleak and I was crying inside. I was going through a traumatic time in my marriage and had gone up to the terrace to be alone and cry in peace. My heart felt like it was breaking and *I wondered if anyone would hear this and come to my rescue.* This was the moment when, for a short space of time, I actually contemplated ending my life. I am not proud of that moment. It was the thought of my son growing up without me that stopped me from taking this extreme step and for that, I am eternally grateful.

At that time, no human help came forward. However, divine help came from within. I realised that we are each in our individual universes, our Gami-Verses. I felt I was being asked by God, "Do you hear when others are suffering? Others around you are also going through their own heaven or hell. Are you able to tap into that? If not, how can you expect others to hear you now?"

I don't know why but somehow this realisation brought me solace. I realised that if any change has to take place, it is up to me. I cannot expect any help from any other human. And I alone was responsible for my life. I cannot assign any blame and I cannot play the victim card. I can only rely on God's wisdom and my inner voice to guide me. I can make my own choices. I can play the victim and be at the receiving end of all the rubbish that was coming my way or I can take steps to create a better life for my son and me. In the subsequent weeks, I started making some small, minute (or nano) decisions about my life, and how I choose to react or not react.

Why do we have our individual universes or Gami-Verses? Why are these different from others? I'm grateful for my Gami-Verse. Imagine your pain and then imagine if you had to take on the pain of others as well. I'm told that enlightened souls are aware of the pain and thoughts of others around them. I have met many such souls and now understand that to take on this power you need a different kind of soul power. To be enlightened involves not just happiness and bliss but also concerns the additional responsibility of others around you and their Gami-Verses. Enlightened saints use their tremendous soul power to take on this additional responsibility while still staying aloof.

Even as a young child, I was surrounded by many saints and enlightened beings. I've been blessed by their association and have seen many miracles manifested in my life and the lives of those around me. These associations did not protect me from hurt but guided me and helped me connect the dots. No one can live your life for you. No one can take away your hurt unless you decide to work on yourself. If it has to be done, it is up to me and up to you as well.

One of the saints I had a fondness for was based in Jalandhar. He was known as Gopal Nagar Babaji, based on the location of his ashram. I don't know his real name, this was what people called him. He could read my thoughts and answer questions that I had not yet fully formulated in my mind. This was during the phase when my soul energy was low and I still needed others to gift me with answers.

He was an enlightened soul and many members of my family would regularly visit him. He would address my aunt as his daughter and I remember longing and yearning for him to call me as his daughter as well. However, I felt my aunt deserved this honour as she was, according to me, at a higher spiritual level and that I was undeserving. It so transpired that my aunt's husband fell seriously ill and she requested me to visit Babaji and get his advice. We had visited him together multiple times with Babaji always calling my aunt his daughter. But on that occasion, he feigned ignorance. He kept questioning me about who I was referring to. I gave him her name, her husband's name, and the name of his business. I urged him to recall the numerous times we had visited him together but to no avail. As a last resort, I informed him that he called her his daughter.

He immediately responded, "Are you too not my daughter?"

I replied with a huge, emphatic yes. That memory still brings a smile to my face. Enlightened souls will always bring about a change in you just with a chance word, a look, or a hint. I have had issues with my father and these incidents actually connected the dots for me, years later, by showering me with love through father figures.

Coming back to the Gami-Verse, I have now understood why we can only live in our own Gami-Verse and can interact with others through their Gami-Verses. The weaker your soul power is, the more involved you are in others' Gami-Verses or dramas. Imagine all souls walking around and living in their unique Gami-Verses. This is similar to the Earth's atmosphere which has layers that surround it and protect it from the harmful rays of the Sun. You are all surrounded by your atmosphere. Your atmosphere is defined by your thoughts, beliefs and self-worth. You attract and deflect your surroundings based on what you have around you. Someone with low self-worth will attract bullies who will drive home the same message. Someone with deep-rooted emotional insecurity and resultant anger issues will attract situations and events that cause them to lose their cool.

Don't even think of escaping from the curated plan of your Gami-Verse. You can escape from something outside you but how can you escape from something within? The role played by your Gami-Verse is to make you stronger, increase your clarity and inculcate a host of qualities. There is no escape route. The sooner you accept the situation around you and understand why you have attracted this, the sooner you can change the functioning of your Gami-Verse and take a step further towards your evolvement.

For example, three people living in the same home will react to the same event differently. One might become philosophical, the other might play the victim card and the third would choose to not get involved in the drama. What is different about them? Their soul power or their Gami-Verses define their reactions. The weaker your soul power, the more you tend to attract and be affected by the drama of others surrounding you. Imagine a stormy sea and a small boat that is getting rocked from all sides. There is a constant state of reaction.

The weaker your atmosphere, the more susceptible you become to outside influences. It's not a question of escapism but having the ability to remain an observer and not get dragged into being a participant. It is this inherent ability that allows individuals with high soul power to not react but observe, analyse, see the big picture and then act as they see fit.

A classic example is people suffering from road rage. They are seated in the air-conditioned comfort of their cars. The cause of their rage is probably a driver in another vehicle who is not even aware of the effect he/she has caused. The person in a rage is constantly reacting to the surrounding circumstances even when others remain unaware. Does this sound familiar? Now recall the times when you have competed with others, maybe while driving or during work, only to later realise that the other person is unaware of your efforts. For instance, you may compete with a colleague. However, you may later realise that they were unaware that they were racing against you. It was all in your head.

How does low soul energy affect you?

Have you ever fasted? Across the world, Muslims observe a fast during the month of Ramzan. For Hindus, the nine days of Navaratri are auspicious and many fast during this time. Christians fast during Lent. Jains fast during Paryushan. The effect of fasting on the body and mind is tremendous and most religions advise it and have incorporated it into their religious practices in some way. Apart from giving the stomach some much-needed rest, self-discipline during fasting empowers the mind. It strengthens one's mind and benefits other areas of one's life too.

As you do anything, so will you do everything.

However, after a fast of 10 days, would you be able to run a marathon? While fasting strengthens the mind, it weakens the body, and it may take a few days to recover. For a strong body, a regular intake of a balanced diet containing proteins, carbohydrates, vitamins and more is essential. You need the fuel given by food to generate the energy in your body. Such 10-day fasts can deplete the fuel that keeps you active and marathon-ready and results in sluggishness. You can compare this with your mobile battery when it has drained to less than 10% charge. The phone then heats up and certain functions are shut down as a defence mechanism to conserve what little charge is left.

If simple things like your phone can showcase the effects of low charge, you can easily imagine the long-term effects of not charging your soul. When your soul has a very low charge, you feel the impact of the heat (circumstances) around you and may curse this effect. You may then constantly look around for energy that can sustain you.

The discharged soul within you is probably crying out for help. How does this play out in your life? You may reach out to others for help. You may get sucked into the dramas created by others. You try to recharge yourself through other people. While seeking energy from others, you forget that they too may be walking around with discharged batteries with no idea how to recharge themselves.

How do you seek energy?

You unconsciously seek this energy through power play, sympathy and gossip, by feeling superior, throwing temper tantrums and many more such scenarios. These play out in your workplace via pressure tactics and blame games. At a personal level, families that have low soul energy will be constantly bickering and abusing each other emotionally and physically. Everyone fights for a slice of the nano energy pie. The little available energy gets passed around to everyone. The weakest member of the family or the team will bear the brunt and will be bullied by other stronger members. These are usually the children. Hence, children growing up in dysfunctional families are the worst affected. As mentioned earlier, the effects of low energy and traumatic events are far higher among children than in adults as they occur during their formative years. An adult who experiences a happy childhood will recover much faster from a traumatic event as an adult as compared to a child who has observed traumatic events happening to their parents or themselves.

I've encountered this many times while coaching people. Events that have taken place when the individual was just four or five years old have affected them more strongly even when they were just observers. Their parents, however, recovered from these events faster and did not recall them very well or had little trauma associated with them. Most psychologists and coaches focus on the inner child and its happiness. You are all still children inside and the hurt that occurred in your childhood defines how you behave as adults. This same hurt also defines the choices and decisions made by you as adults.

When you walk around with low soul energy, you get affected by everyone around you. You are all aware of the depletion of the ozone layer resulting in harmful ultraviolet rays reaching the earth. Similarly, low soul energy creates a weak atmosphere around you and you become more prone to being affected and getting involved in everything happening around you. How this energy gets pulled, snatched and stolen will be covered later.

You are all beings filled with energy. Low soul energy levels create individuals who are quick to blame and point fingers at others for every problem in their lives. They will always play the victim card. How can you identify such individuals?

Look out for the following behaviours:

- Displaying temper tantrums or road rage
- Fighting and blaming others for their behaviour
- Always feeling like victims
- Feeling burdened with no capacity to handle anything extra

- Always seeking sympathy or acceptance from others
- Always irritated
- Exhibiting attention-seeking behaviour and using curse words or provoking others
- Wanting others to support them financially
- Looking for the easy way out
- Being jealous of the others' achievements
- Seeking success without hard work
- Always comparing themselves to others
- Giving up easily with no resilience or capacity to handle rejection or failures
- Changing professions or jobs constantly, in the hope that the next one will be better
- Unable to handle change
- Lacking the capacity to learn more with no flexibility or acceptance of anything new
- Turning small incidents into monumental dramas
- Harbouring suicidal thoughts or actions

If you are a parent operating on low soul energy, you cannot instil high soul energy in your children. I've attended many PTA meetings when my son was in school and I've observed parents fighting with teachers to get their child's grade up by a few marks. Instead of appreciating the work done by teachers, their focus is on how the marks can be increased.

It's not just a question of marks. They are deriving their energy from dominating the teacher. What role models are they creating for their children, where a teacher who should be respected looks incompetent? Children grow up accepting that blaming others is the norm. Instead of the talk being directed to what more can be done, what are the areas of improvement in the child, and what can the teacher and parent achieve together, the focus is on something minor such as marks and grades.

I remember attending these meetings and discussing the areas where my child needed to improve. I appreciated the honest feedback I received from the teacher so that I could focus on these areas with my child. Before every exam or test, the focus would be on achievement and after the test result, the focus was on acceptance.

I'm happy that I have been able to accept failure, and achieve resilience rather than crying to get some wrong corrected. I have chosen to achieve on my own terms and not by something that is handed to me as a result of my complaint. Wanting the best for my child also had me praying for his failure. My son is an above-average and highly intelligent individual. Hence, as a child, he did not feel the need to apply himself to his studies. As he entered college, it became a game for him. How many days before the exam should he purchase the books? He became overconfident and I did not see this ending well. As a parent, I was worried and actually started praying for his failure. I knew that only his failures could teach him resilience. Furthermore, this would be a less painful lesson if learnt as a child or teenager as compared to as an adult. As an adult, I couldn't guarantee a support system for him but if he learnt this when he was young, I knew I could support him and guide him through it.

My prayers were answered when he failed the CA (Chartered Accountancy) entrance CPT (Common Proficiency Test). I supported him and questioned the effort that needed to be made and how he could plan his studies better. Although disheartened, he did not give up and cleared the CPT on his second attempt with 157/200. The passing marks were 100. He cleared his CA-IPCC (mid-levels) in three attempts and achieved 60 and above in three papers out of eight. This is called achieving an exemption. You don't need to give the entire group of papers again. You can only give the individual papers and achieve over 40. His never-give-up spirit got a boost during his repeated attempts. Believe me, I took more pride in his spirit than his marks. He achieved something larger than clearing his CA-IPCC. He learnt to accept failure, achieve resilience, and grow into someone I admire and respect.

His marks made me happy but my chief source of pride was his ability to overcome failure, build resilience, and keep trying. These failures transformed him from a casual and overconfident teenager to a resilient and courageous person. I believe that the way he added these qualities to his Gami-Verse shaped his qualities as an adult.

In a professional scenario, when managers operate on low soul energy, they cannot create high-energy teams. Their time is spent on firefighting and managing chaos instead of innovating, creating, and foreseeing potential problems.

I was privileged to work with managers who had high energy and also those who had low soul energy. While

I've done my best work with high-energy leaders, who encouraged, challenged, and inspired me; I've also learnt a lot while working with people who had low energy. They taught me how to remain aloof and not get sucked into their web, how to sustain my energy, create my own space, and deliver a good performance despite their sub-standard managerial style.

I call the managerial style of low-energy managers as chaos management. Have you worked under someone who gets easily riled up? As managers, they are meant to guide but are instead in a constant state of upheaval. There is no end to the problems they face. They are always the victim. There is no talk or negligible talk on future planning. If there is future planning and goals are set, there is little or no follow-up for implementation. A bare minimum of goals are implemented just to ensure that work gets done. For the most part, the focus is on fighting daily fires and being on the receiving end of all the upheaval created by others. I repeat, managing chaos.

You can identify the working style of low-energy managers through the following indicators:

- No clear definition of roles within the team
- Even when roles are defined, these keep getting mixed based on the current emergency
- Deadlines keep getting pushed back
- Work schedules are completed only when completely essential
- Deadlines decide the work getting completed

- There are too many meetings and time spent on them is not productive
- Too many questions and too few answers
- Delay in decision-making
- Decisions taken are related to current emergencies and not based on future planning
- Teams feel dissatisfied with the work achieved
- More focus on keeping the boss happy
- Always being a victim and facing the brunt from all sides
- No time for innovation or forward planning
- None or minimum concentration on strategies or analysis
- No clear succession planning within the team
- Anyone with leadership qualities is discouraged and all new ideas rejected
- Oversharing of ideas by the manager creates distrust within the team

Managers whose souls have low energy cannot create leaders under them. To create leaders, you need an environment of innovation, idea discussion, and decision-making.

You can also identify such individuals through the following indicators:

- Always blaming others

- Always stressing how much others should be grateful to them
- Always having issues with their family, their team or the company they work for. They will always have some people who they are biased against.
- Always manipulating others to their point of view
- Always needing power over others, and showcasing this power using their money or knowledge.
- Against accommodating others' views or feelings
- Unwilling or with no capacity to handle any burden

Furthermore, such individuals lack the ability to handle failures. Their talk will always be centred around failures and not on 'What next?' There is zero or minimum resilience. Even small incidents create monumental dramas. You can always identify such individuals by the length of their sob stories. They will give you their entire history along with the length and breadth of their misfortune. The focus on recovery and what they learnt is less than what they have experienced.

One of my mentors, Blair Singer, used to say, "Short Story, Large Message." This only happens when you use the experience you have undergone as a stepping stool towards understanding or unlocking another area of your mind and overcoming another challenge. High soul energy individuals will focus less on the event that has taken place in their lives and more on the learning they have received from the event. They assimilate the learning and move beyond the actual event. They use the event as a stepping stone and start connecting the dots on why they experienced this and what they are learning from it. It's not surprising that the ratio of talk to learning will be higher. High soul energy individuals will be focused on what they have learnt and what else they can plan.

What do you do when your energy is low? You constantly and subconsciously seek energy from your surroundings or the people around you. There is a constant narrative happening within you that you are not worthy, you can't do this, what will people say, and how many problems surround you. This internal talk focuses only on problems and not on solutions.

As per the data published by the National Crime Records Bureau (NCRB) on Accidental Deaths & Suicides in India (2021), the number of suicides in India has increased from 1,29,887 in 2017 to 1,64,033 in 2021.

List-2.1
Number of Suicides, Growth of Population and Rate of Suicides during 2017 - 2021

Sl. No.	Year	Total Number of Suicides	Mid-Year Projected Population (in Lakh*)	Rate of Suicides (Col.3/Col.4)
(1)	(2)	(3)	(4)	(5)
1	2017	129,887	13,091.6#	9.9
2	2018	134,516	13,233.8#	10.2
3	2019	139,123	13,376.1#	10.4
4	2020	153,052	13,533.9$	11.3
5	2021	164,033	13,671.8$	12.0

Source: https://ncrb.gov.in/sites/default/files/ADSI-2021/adsi2021_Chapter-2-Suicides.pdf

Source: Report of the Technical Group on Population Projections (November, 2019), National Commission on Population, Ministry of Health & Family Welfare.

$ Source: Report of the Technical Group on Population Projections (July, 2020), National Commission on Population, Ministry of Health & Family Welfare.

There is a clear indication that the despondency felt by people is on the rise. The world that you live in is more advanced than in the last century. You have seen the Industrial Revolution, the Information Technology Revolution, and now the Digital Revolution. There are now a record number of hospitals, healers, advisors, consultants, analysts, and all manner of specialists available and they are growing. Why then are the cases of mental, emotional, and physical ill health on the rise? If physical health is an indicator, the number of people focusing on their health is also on the rise. The number of gymnasiums, dietitians, and fitness instructors today is phenomenal. You can see content being posted every second on YouTube advising everyone on all aspects of health.

With no dearth of information, why then are disorders like depression, anxiety, panic attacks and heart attacks also on the rise? Hospitals are overflowing with patients. People are facing burnout, looking for release through any means possible. The sheer number of pubs today is much more than seen in the past. The number of spiritual gurus, healers, guides, astrologers, and tarot card readers is also increasing. People are even looking towards the occult and the paranormal for answers.

I remember reading a book by one of my favourite authors, Georgette Heyer. The book entitled 'A Civil Contract' had the following lines: "*It was only in epic tragedies that gloom was unrelieved. In real life, tragedy and comedy were so intermingled that when one was most wretched, ridiculous things happened to make one laugh in spite of oneself.*"

As humans, you will go through emotional highs and lows. While there are times when you go through stress, these are relieved by periods of laughter, happiness, and peace. All things get balanced out. Or do they? With the growing number of suicides and depression on the rise, it is a clear indicator that people are operating in a constant state of darkness.

With all the development the world has seen, it ought to be a better place, however, it is actually in its darkest phase. The variety of choices available to humans is amazing and could not have been imagined even 100 years ago. The amount of wealth and prosperity in the world has also increased. There has been a rise in the number of billionaires.

The last decade has seen so many singers and performers who were at the peak of their careers commit suicide, get addicted, or suffer from depression and take medicines for it. It is not poverty or a lack of options that is creating this darkness within them. Addiction to gaming and mobile phones has also increased. You can see this all around you. Even at parties, people are constantly on their phones, sometimes just playing games. They disconnect from the people around them and try to escape into a make-believe world of scores and levels.

These games are very addictive. I had started playing games on my mobile when my job was at its most stressful. A couple of games I enjoyed had daily levels that you needed to cross. While I had limited my time on achieving new levels, it had become second nature to me to play this game at least once a day, to complete the daily challenge and close the app. At one time, I realised that I had played the game daily for more than two years. I was inordinately proud of this achievement. I also deluded myself by thinking that the game was stretching my mind and that this was something that would help me. I have come to realise that any online game that makes your brain function faster will sap your soul energy. In essence, playing these games decreased my concentration and focus levels.

While overcoming my addiction to television and comfort food took time, my addiction to the mobile was the most difficult to overcome. Till today I find myself slipping back. While I do not have any games on my phone or laptop, I still find myself being drawn to YouTube and TV. However, it's a conscious thought now and not a daily occurrence. I have taken measures that have reduced this temptation to a mere fraction of what it was.

Furthermore, everyone expects all answers to come from outside. They have locked up their inner voice so deeply within them that not even a sliver of it is ever heard again. People flock to saints and godmen/women for their answers. They are looking for external solutions to their physical, mental and even emotional ailments. All emotional outbursts are blamed on others. YOU made me angry. YOU are to blame. Why did YOU make me lose my temper? YOU are the reason for my depression. Everyone is looking to assign the blame on others.

I remember seeing the movie 'About Time' where humans have a limited amount of time left and are constantly seeking time from others by purchasing, begging or stealing it. There is a similar pursuit taking place currently for answers, for peace, and for relief from the darkness.

What has created this need for everyone to be constantly doing something? The frenzy that I associated with the rat race is replaced with everyone wanting to be distracted and not wanting to hear their inner voice. They don't want to stop and want to escape from themselves. They are overstimulated by the shiny things that surround them. This is similar to a cranky child who's not ready to sleep and wants to be entertained or distracted at all costs.

If you try to find solace from outside, then everything has an entertainment value. You may have even compromised with good, nutritional, and healthy food and replaced it with fast food that provides comfort.

You look around you for cheap thrills to sustain you. The rise in gaming, gambling, alcoholism, drug use, casual sex, and addiction to social media that you are observing today is due to this. You may have never seen this in your world before. You will find people crossing the road, glued to their mobiles, and attending training sessions on their mobiles. A simple walk is now a walk with a constant stream of songs blasting directly into your ears through your headphones. I've even seen people watching television while playing games on their mobile.

Television channels too have progressed from showing news to participating in gossip. Everything has become 'Breaking News.' In India, this is called *sansani khabar* (sensational news). Every channel is promoting this. Even while viewing the news, you will keep track of not just what is unfolding on the main screen but multiple tickers or rolling news items that are playing at the bottom of the screen, mostly in a loop. The frenzy is everywhere.

There are Indian TV serials that have been going on for ages without a break. They were extremely popular. They were called *saas-bahu* (mother-in-law and daughter-in-law) serials. People would be glued to the screen from 8 pm to almost 11 pm. These shows were also repeated the next morning. I actually knew people who would watch the episodes at night and the repeats too. They would then call up their family and friends and discuss the happenings like it was news.

The news channels caught up with this trend. Imagine my surprise when one of the Indian channels launched a news program called *Saas Bahu aur Sazish* (mother-in-law, daughter-in-law and machinations). They would create news out of the stories shown on television. People started watching these too.

Everyone is constantly hunting for the next dose of entertainment. The addiction levels are at an all-time high. They want entertainment from food, news, and social media with more content and they want it faster whereas weekends are for partying. There are excuses made for excessive alcohol consumption, gossiping, and drugs. Everyone is looking for happiness outside and not within. They want to be seen, and want likes and validation from others.

During my corporate stint, I would take my team and associates out for lunch two to three times a year. During one such lunch, I noticed that one of my team members would take a picture of each dish served, post it on her social media and then commence eating. This was a regular restaurant and not fine dining. The food was presented ordinarily, there was nothing special. However, she seemed to constantly need validation for the food she was eating. Her enjoyment of the food was dependent on the amount of likes she garnered over the meal. This trend has grown only recently.

Once, while giving some of the girls from work a lift, we crossed a pub. They asked me to stop the car right outside. The three girls in the backseat took a selfie and posted the pic on social media stating that they were enjoying girl time at the pub. This blew my mind. Was social validation so important that people had to fake enjoyment? I realised later that just like the person who fasts for several days gets weakened physically, the soul is famished due to lack of nourishment. Energy is being derived not from within but from external sources through the perception of what will get the individual noticed. Such people live through the power gained from the reaction of others and their association with those who they believe are more powerful. They imitate others to project an image of power and believe that the projected image is the true one. They then create a make-believe world around that false image. They do not try to strengthen the soul but project a false sense of power hoping to make them feel powerful.

You are moving away from your inner voice and hoping to get the answers from outside. Where does this end? The world around you keeps trying to find new ways to mess with your mind and to shift you from being laid back to leaning forward. I keep getting suggestions on YouTube to expedite my viewing to 1.5x. You have all types of short-form content available. Even Whatsapp promises to expedite voice messages to 1.5x. What is happening to the world? Within the three volumes of E-volvement, I promise you that you will receive all your answers. You will realise how change is in your own hands. You have to all make this conscious effort to choose the path of evolvement.

You are all energy seekers

When the soul's self-generated energy levels are low, it unconsciously looks around for ways in which its energy can be replenished. You keep looking at others who are more successful and have achieved more in life. Today's world is obsessed with knowing everyone's net worth. There are numbers attached to each achievement. These numbers become milestones for others to aspire to.

Movies are not being rated for the story, their music, their content or even the % of profit received but whether they are part of the 100 Cr or 200 Cr club. Achieving 100 Cr immediately validates the efforts of the director and producer and showcases their success to the world. If this is the only yardstick, then why are these successful overachievers depressed? They have achieved cult status but are still in pain internally and are battling depression and anxiety.

Everyone is seeking energy from others around them. This energy comes from showing off, seeking attention, gaining sympathy, conning others, and bullying them. Energy is gained but it is temporary and fleeting in nature. Why is that? You fail to realise that you are seeking energy to fuel your souls from others who are energy stealers and not energy generators. Everyone around you is moving around in this semi-depleted state. While you aim to obtain energy from other depleted souls, you don't achieve your daily requirement.

Have you heard of the proverb, 'An apple a day keeps the doctor away'? Imagine yourself eating only one apple a day and nothing else. Or imagine you are eating only one slice of an apple and expecting complete physical, mental, and emotional health. Now imagine eating only one slice of the apple not just for one day but for the last 10, 20 or 30 years. How do you feel about this? Do you think your energy levels would be high with this limited diet? Do you feel this diet of one slice will sustain you? If this is not enough for a human being to survive and keep the physical body healthy, can you relate to what happens to your soul with minimal or no nourishment?

What does a depleted soul do?

Have you experienced what happens to your mobile phone when its battery is low?

All of you use your mobiles as a lifeline. I don't know about you but I have transferred all my details to my phone and my survival depends on it. It's an important part of my being and I need it to be fully charged to live my life. So what happens when the charge reaches below the danger level? When it reaches 20% or below, the phone starts heating up. Even basic tasks slow down. The phone reminds you to seek out a charging point to restore its energy levels and to shore up resources if you want it to function at optimum levels. At a 10% charge, the connection to the internet also shuts down. Communication with the outside world exists at a bare minimum. Just because your soul does not have a warning light, it has been easy for you to ignore its need. When there is a low charge, what does your soul do? It starts heating up. It gets affected by everything that is happening around it.

How do you recognise someone with a low soul charge?

Listen to the people around you. Start identifying the ones who are the whiners, the complainers, the criers, and the blamers. The more vocal people, the ones who always vent out their problems and have issues with the world, are the ones with less charge or energy. Low charging is also visible when there is a lot of anxiety, panic attacks, and feelings of being overburdened. If you compare the soul's Gami-Verse to the earth's atmosphere, then the more depleted the soul, the more holes there are in the ozone layer. The soul lacks the protection of a good layer of energy and is affected by everything that's happening around it. Every single thing that is happening gets hoarded. This is its default defence mechanism.

What does a depleted soul hoard?

It hoards all events that can hurt. When the soul's atmosphere is depleted, every event that is not positive hurts. These can include its association with experienced trauma, lack of understanding, absence of love, and paucity of choices. Even small obligations create burdens.

Not getting that raise at work? It hurts.

Not being appreciated? It hurts.

Not receiving love? It hurts.

Being insulted? It hurts.

Not being heard? It hurts.

Not getting sympathy? It hurts.

Not getting likes on social media? It hurts.

Getting unfollowed on Instagram? It hurts.

That's not all. In the current scenario, students facing an educational challenge feel trauma, panic, and despondency. Similarly, any business challenge creates trauma and panic.

What starts off as something small starts collecting until you have a reservoir or collection of hurts and traumas. It's not just one thing but everything and present everywhere. Most people will do one of these things when faced with this gigantic collection: they will externalise this hurt by being vocal, raging and having a short temper that explodes at every turn or they will internalise it and feel despondent, depressed or gloomy.

Does any of this sound familiar? During my corporate career, I would regularly travel on the Mumbai local train. Everyone around me used to be stressed out. They had hair-trigger tempers and I was careful to not offend anyone for fear of nasty repercussions. To enter or exit from the train was a task and eight times out of 10, somebody would complain. I would witness people around complaining about their jobs, their spouses, their in-laws, and much more.

During my early days, I remember not receiving the raise I was promised. It felt like my entire universe had shifted. I felt hurt and cheated. What I most specifically remember during that time is not just the feeling but the oversharing of my disappointment. I would pour out the entire recital of hurt to all my colleagues, family, and friends. I'm not happy with that part of my past but am sharing it here. I am just as human as each one of you and not someone who will keep quiet. I was upset and ensured that everyone I met was aware of how I was cheated. I blamed others and placed myself in the victim zone. This zone is the easiest to fall into. It may happen to all of you, even the best of you.

I realised only later that by choosing to be a victim, I was inviting more problems into my life. Victims will always be reactive. They will always be at the receiving end and will blame everyone except themselves.

A victim gets angry because of others.

A victim gets irritated because of others.

A victim gets hurt because of others.

A victim gets cheated because of others.

A victim stays a victim even when he/she/they find success.

A victim will always present himself or herself as blameless and dependent on others. Victims seek sympathy from their surroundings and gravitate naturally to those who dole out the maximum amount of this coveted sentiment.

A client I was briefly working with, Amit (name changed), had converted this habit into an art form. He blamed his mother for her squeaky voice. He blamed her nagging for the physical abuse he directed towards her. For a time, I too believed him and felt that he had been wronged. His sister and mother had started him on schizophrenia treatment when, according to him, he was just exploring his spiritual inclinations. After 12 years of medication, his memory and behaviour were affected. He had lost his father when he was 8 years old. I realised how deep-rooted his sense of being a victim was when, at the age of 34, he still blamed his father for not guiding him towards a spiritual or religious mindset. I realised his sense of being was defined by his feeling of victimisation and this was the reason he could never complete any project or work towards anything concrete. He thrived by making his family live in this constant state of guilt.

This was an unorthodox case for me. I had been approached to work with him by his sister. This was one client where I had gone against my principles and accepted him though he had not hired me himself. During my discovery call with him, I felt that I could help him and I tried. However, I later realised that he was not accountable as he was not paying for my services. I tried to challenge him to get him out of his victim mindset and gave him a chance to prove his sincerity. He chose to continue with his thinking and revelled in being a victim. I was happy when he chose to end our sessions.

His circumstances had created a victim mentality within him. What was initially just an event had become an integral part of his being.

The ability to continue reliving traumatic events and not moving forward is the identifying trait of a depleted soul. I've seen some hoarders who accumulate physical things. They fill up every square inch of their homes and are comfortable only when they have limited space to move. The sheer amount of physical matter in their homes creates a sense of comfort for them. It's not how most others would choose to live. While a physical hoarder is easy to spot, an emotional hoarder cannot be easily identified.

Some easy-to-spot traits of an emotional hoarder are given below.

- Will hold a grudge and consequently always think of themselves as victims
- Always sharing their hurts via long and torturous stories
- Always in reactive mode
- Short-tempered
- Irritable
- Moody
- Feeling despondent
- Addicted
- No sense of gratitude
- Wanting change but not doing anything to achieve it
- Having a feeling of self-entitlement
- Not giving but always taking
- Presenting several excuses for their bad behaviour

How does living with a depleted and energy-stealing soul affect you?

Neha (name changed) was someone I had coached. At that time, one of the areas that she had been struggling with was handling her roommate Priya (name changed). This had been a major concern for her and she felt incapable of asking Priya to leave. She had taken her in because she had felt sorry for her. We delved into Neha's reasons for taking on this relationship and during our sessions, she did resolve it and stand up for herself. I remember asking Neha the following questions about her roommate and here are her answers to them.

- You say that Priya is going through a tough phase and that you have helped her out. However, does she display gratitude?

o On a scale of 1 to 10, 10 being the most grateful and 1 being ungrateful, Priya was a 1.

- If you were in Priya's place and someone had helped you out in a similar manner, how grateful would you be?

o On a scale of 1 to 10, 10 being the most grateful and 1 being ungrateful, I would be a 10. I would probably help out with house chores, and find ways to repay the kind gesture.

- Does Priya care for you like you care for her?

o No. Priya is always going on about how she has nowhere to go. She doesn't have anyone to care for her.

- Does Priya help around the house?

o Priya doesn't help around the house. She spends her time watching television.

- As you have allowed her to share your room, who has taken more space?

o It's Priya. She has moved in and spread her stuff everywhere. She also has a dog who needs to be looked after. She invites her boyfriend to stay over. Priya sleeps till late and I have to tiptoe around to not disturb her.

- Would your family and friends, who care for you, approve of Priya?

o I had already been recommended by my family and close friends to end this toxic, one-sided relationship.

- If you had not heard her entire sob story and just had knowledge of her habits and actions, would you have ever befriended Priya or allowed her into your home?

o A definite no.

Have you experienced such toxic relationships? Some relationships you choose may become toxic later but some are ones you may grow into.

I recollect a somewhat similar case of someone from a wealthy family who was looking after other poor relations. Guilt is a big driver for attracting toxic relationships. If you feel guilty because you have more resources, you may overcompensate by taking on others who are less privileged. In this particular case, Abha (name changed) had not attracted this relationship. She was from the third generation of a wealthy family. Her grandparents had felt sorry for their poorer relations and had started the practice of looking after them. We later realised that the help had continued over the last 5 decades. Why were the dependents not supporting themselves yet?

I have found such examples in my family too. There are some relationships that we inherit. I belong to a family that is big on philanthropy and I assumed that it was our duty to look after the less privileged. I realised much later that one cannot help someone who gets spoilt due to the support. The help should not create a false sense of entitlement in others and make them complacent and ready to extend their begging bowl. The realisation that the aunt and cousins that I loved belonged to this category was tough. My moment of realisation occurred when we had helped them during a major medical emergency. We had gone out of our way and slashed our household budget. The family had also received help from other sources and they used the money left over after expenses to purchase a car. They justified the car by saying that their son had insisted and they couldn't refuse. We ceased supporting them and, within a few years, they became affluent. What had not been possible for at least two decades was suddenly a reality. The cherry on the cake was that they started flaunting their wealth with no thought of repaying what they had been given earlier. All the help that we had provided was taken by them as their right.

This realisation was an important one for me. The guilt of being privileged cannot make me spoil someone else. The *karma* attached to this deed would be mine. I alone would be responsible for someone else's laziness. Cutting off the supply will actually spur them to become self-reliant.

Over the years we have helped numerous families through giving *daswandh*. This is a part of the Sikh tradition of keeping aside 10% of your income to help the underprivileged. The money donated is not from our wallet but from the *daswandh* (God's bank) managed by us. The rule of 10% is a healthy way of giving money and saves us from the negative *karma* associated with the receiver not being worthy of our help. This is the best way of giving donations. However, we now follow a checklist.

- Is this help temporary in nature or does it look like it is becoming permanent?
- What is the receiver doing to ensure such a scenario does not occur again?
- Are you spoiling the habits of the receiver?
- Is the receiver embarrassed to receive this help or has he/she become comfortable with asking?

While I don't wish that anyone should be embarrassed to ask for help, this is an important yardstick. There have been many people whom we have helped as a family over the years. Genuine receivers are always grateful. They try in their own way to compensate for the help and also realise that they must try to limit their requirements.

The above checklist will help you separate the genuinely needy individuals from the fake ones. Differentiate the energy stealers from the energy givers. These people might be unprivileged but will still retain their energy and not be toxic to you. Being aware of the emotional manipulation by energy stealers is half the battle won and sob stories will no longer move you. You can just take a step back and analyse how their story affects you. You can check if their actions and behaviours match their words. If you have attracted such toxic relationships in your life, you are most likely surrounded by weak souls. It's not that you will find such weak souls only among the underprivileged and needy. You may find many of these energy stealers in your professional life too. The power wielders manipulate their team emotionally for their purposes. This is a type of energy stealing too. I have been privileged to watch some of these master manipulators in action. I have observed first-hand the effect that connecting with them has on others.

Energy stealers can come in many forms. The effect on you is always the same. There will be a feeling of being unhappy, confusion (this takes place because the visible narrative is different from the invisible one taking place), and feeling depleted after a meeting. You may also feel a lack of empowerment, a feeling of helplessness, or being overburdened. There will also be an increase in the levels of anxiety, panic attacks and stress-related ailments. This has been rightly defined by my mentor Ron Malhotra as 'What surrounds us gets inside us'.

The sheer number of depleted and weak souls that are present today has never been seen earlier in this world though it has seen physical hardships, wars, and lack of medical help. In the present day, the number of mental illness cases continue to be on the rise.

Unhealthy work cultures, toxic relationships, energy stealers, depleted souls looking at other depleted souls for sustenance and a lack of soul power to overcome trauma and hurt—all these have contributed towards the rising epidemic of mental illness.

An article by the World Health Organization (WHO) published on 17 June 2022 highlights the urgent need to transform mental health and mental health care.[1] An extract from the article states: In 2019, nearly a billion people—including 14% of the world's adolescents—were living with a mental disorder. Suicide accounted for more than 1 in 100 deaths and 58% of suicides occurred before the age of 50. Mental disorders are the leading cause of disability, causing 1 in 6 years lived with disability. People with severe mental health conditions die on average 10 to 20 years earlier than the general population, mostly due to preventable physical diseases. Childhood sexual abuse and victimisation through bullying are major causes of depression. Social and economic inequalities, public health emergencies, war, and the climate crisis are among the global and structural threats to mental health. Depression and anxiety went up by more than 25% in the first year of the pandemic alone. The number of hospitals has grown exponentially. The research in medical science has been phenomenal. The world is more prosperous today as compared to the last century. There are more choices available. Why then are the number of mentally ill patients rising?

Another extract from Statista is given below.[2]

---

[1] https://www.who.int/news/item/17-06-2022-who-highlights-urgent-need-to-transform-mental-health-and-mental-health-care#:~:text=In%202019%2C%20nearly%20a%20billion,6%20years%20lived%20with%20disability

[2] https://www.statista.com/topics/6944/mental-health-in-india/#editorsPicks

Depression, stress, and anxiety

In India, every seventh person suffers from some form of mental disorder. The epidemiology of mental disorders, specifically depression, has been vastly studied on a global scale. Today, it is regarded as the leading contributor to disease burden and morbidity worldwide, which may even result in suicide if left untreated.

What is stealing of soul energy and how is it related to bullying of adults?

My first introduction to the stealing of soul energy was around 2004 through the book 'The Celestine Prophecy' by James Redfield. The book contained a total of nine insights; the third and fourth insights made an enormous impact on me. The third one, **A Matter of Energy**, spoke of your entire world as an energy field that you can control with your thoughts. The fourth one called **Struggle for Power** brought up the entire concept of how humans fight for power. As per the book, each of us has our own dramas, relationships or circumstances that have created a life pattern within us, thereby controlling us. While these life patterns define our reactions, they also bring to light areas of our life where we are able to easily sustain our energy as opposed to areas where we allow others to steal this. This was an entirely new concept and I could relate this to certain areas of my life.

While I received unconditional love from my mother, my father was a whole different ball game. I was being constantly compared to everyone else in every area of my life. Someone was better at sports and someone else was better at studies. Someone could walk or run better. Someone else could cycle better. Someone else made better choices. I was even compared unfavourably with my little sister who was seven years younger than me. She, it seems, was luckier for my father. As a child, I suffered from febrile convulsions and was a sickly child. I imagine I was not an ideal child but these unfavourable comparisons wounded me and I was always struggling for approval. I was the dutiful child who accepted whatever my father said unconditionally without analysing whether he was right or wrong.

When I first read The Celestine Prophecy, I had separated from my emotionally abusive husband and had chosen to end my six-year marriage. As a single parent living with my parents, I was trying to overcome depression, create a new career for myself and rebuild my life. Over the years, all my negative thoughts and coping mechanisms have created further health issues for me. Some healing has taken place already while other aspects are still a work in progress. But what has worked for me and has transformed my life completely will surely work for you all. My purpose in sharing my story is not to gain your sympathy but to assure you that these methods work. My only hope is you do not struggle with this endlessly and evolve yourselves within a short span of a few years.

I realised, after reading the book, that the drama created by my father was not due to anything that my mother or I had done. It was his coping mechanism due to his low energy. He had chosen the easiest path to survive by stealing our energy and becoming powerful. It is very easy to oppress those whom we love and are closely related to. Others would not allow you this power or would block you in an instant. It is only close family that will always bear the brunt of bullying and energy stealing. My energy was repeatedly stolen as a child by my father and later as an adult by my ex-husband.

The victim creates the bully. This happens because of our easy acceptance of the bully in our lives, by not blocking the energy stealing, not creating roadblocks and anti-viruses and by allowing these robbers to enter our energy field and steal at will. As a homeowner, do you leave the front door and windows of your home wide open and accept that anyone can come in and steal at will? If you don't, then why does this differ when it comes to your energy field? Just because it is invisible doesn't make it less tangible. How had I allowed others to invade my space, treat me badly and rule over me?

The Celestine Prophecy showed me a path to recovery but the process was my own. It took me some time to assimilate my situation, to understand how energy actually works, and to realise how my energy was stolen. We will cover these in detail in volume 2 of the E-volvement trilogy in the section covering the five koshas.

However, there is one thing that I did then and still do when faced with an energy stealer. I take a mental step back while calmly repeating in my mind, "I'm not giving you this energy. I have created this energy. It's mine and mine alone. You do not have the right to steal it and use it to feel powerful." Outwardly my face remains calm and this is the result of the inner calm that is created when you have successfully protected your energy. The remote control of your life continues to stay in your hands. I'm indebted to James Redfield's book for providing me with this solution.

I can now claim to have used this successfully and have grown exponentially in life by utilising MY ENERGY for MY NEEDS.

Long-term exposure to energy stealers and adult bullies is equal to a university-level education. I do not think any university could have provided me with this life-changing experience. Over the years it became my agenda to not just protect my energy but to generate, grow, and learn every aspect of this vital resource and to understand how the world is struggling for soul energy. What are the ways in which people try to steal energy? What happens when you try to steal energy from pure souls? What kind of *karma* gets created?

Are you aware that like addicts who need the next fix, energy stealers are the biggest addicts? They are constantly in search of their next big fix. They are not able to generate energy and have become used to getting it easily from others. They surround themselves with people whom they can suck dry. It's like having an energy drink with the straw ready for easy access. Here are some of the narratives used by them:

- Why do YOU do this?
- Why do YOU make me angry?
- Can't YOU see that I'm upset?
- Can't YOU understand basic things?
- How are YOU so dumb?
- Why can't YOU remember these things?
- Why do I have to keep reminding YOU?

I had the great opportunity to work with a master energy stealer. There were some 8-10 people in the team reporting to him. Over the years, he had gotten used to utilising two people in his team as his guaranteed source of energy. I had to work closely with one of these sources. It was interesting and once I became aware of the energy stealing and protected myself, I just watched. Let's call the victim Danny. For every mistake I made, Danny was held accountable. I reported directly to the big boss himself but every area where change was required was routed through Danny to me. There was more to it.

Every achievement of mine was weaponised to blame Danny. "See how much she has done. Why can't you do this?"

I remember we were placing certain policies for approval before certain board-level committees. I knew when these were scheduled and sent a reminder to my manager. As a result, he was able to attend the meeting.

This too was blamed on Danny. "See how she reminded me. Why couldn't you do that?"

It was not just me. Every issue was blamed on Danny. He was meant to be this omnipresent being who could foresee everything and handle everything. Over the years, the relationship between these two became so toxic that Danny actually became ineffective from all the energy loss. The big boss himself while constantly blaming Danny was addicted to him and could not distance himself. Like addicts require a fix in the form of the things they are addicted to, energy addicts get addicted to certain people and situations. They will blame them, control them, constantly rebuke them, hurt them, and abuse them but still want them around.

This is why abusers want their victims around them. They will always apologise for their behaviour and actions after the event. They will emotionally blackmail their victims and manipulate them through any means possible. They keep their victims around like energy drinks, with a supply of ready energy to be sucked out at will.

In the book 'Show Your Work' by Austin Kleon, there is a chapter on 'The Vampire Test.' He refers to the biography by John Richardson 'A Life of Picasso' which mentions Picasso's penchant for sucking the energy out of all the people he met. People would have a great time around Picasso and then later go home nervous and exhausted. He, on the other hand, would use this energy and spend the night painting in his studio. While Picasso used this energy to create masterpieces, most people use it to survive. Bullies lack a good self-image and need this to feel powerful. Energy stealers are bullies in their personal space and lord over people they have the most control over. These will include their spouse, children, aged parents, servants, or neighbours. In a professional arena, these will include their team, vendors, or associates over whom they have control. A business owner might delay payment towards a consultant just to show his power and may want the consultant to approach and beg him.

My personal experience of bullying was that of my ex-husband. During my six-year marriage, I too was the recipient of many such tactics. I wasn't happy in my marriage. There was no respect, only adjustments that I alone had to make. At the time, my concept of abuse was physical abuse. I did not understand emotional abuse. He did raise his hand a few times but I countered this. I was firm that he could not treat me like this. The amount of emotional abuse that was being doled out was beyond my understanding. It was many many years later that I realised there is a term for this: gaslighting. It started off at a very subtle level. I was gently told about how others were talking about me. All the friends I made were apparently talking about me behind my back. I was being made fun of. My sense of self-worth was destroyed gradually so that the only support I would turn to would be my husband.

I remember seeing the Netflix series 'Maid'. The protagonist was asked by the authorities whether she was abused. She replies, "No." The only abuse you readily associate with is physical violence. The emotional abuse had never been highlighted before. For most people, this behaviour is acceptable and is a part of life. They might complain but will do nothing to change the status quo. What actions are being taken to change the situation? If this is a repeated offence, are you then not responsible for this offence by your inaction? Should you encourage such behaviour or should you condemn it? Should you let others continue their offence by not shoring up your defence? At the end of the day, are you not responsible for ensuring your well-being?

You alone are responsible for the bullies in your life—the people in your family, neighbourhood, and office who believe it's okay to steal your energy. They ensure that they always have the last word, always dominate every conversation, and never let others progress. They need validation of their success through the failures of others and are always looking for your sympathy, but their actions do not show their gratitude.

How can you protect yourself from these energy stealers or vampires? How can you recognise these bullies in your life? There are multiple types of bullies and you will not find all these traits in the same person. However, you will definitely find three or more characteristics from the list below that will enable you to identify them.

1. Bullies will unnecessarily raise their voices in the middle of a conversation. This is not done to speak passionately but instead to silence other voices.

2. Bullies will dominate every conversation. They always have the last word, whether in personal interactions, through telephonic conversation, WhatsApp or email. They will display what I call verbal or email diarrhoea. While they are having the last word, they won't care for anyone interrupting them. They will flood the conversation with their pronouncements and may also bring up long-forgotten matters/other occurrences and link them to the current conversation even when they are not relevant.

3. They will blow hot and cold. They will be extremely sweet and pleasant at times and extremely volcanic at others. People affected by bullies and present in the range of their energy intake will mirror their behaviour. They will be happy and relieved when the bully is pleasant and quake when they are angry. Even the thought of facing these bullies will make others

around them tremble. They enumerate a master and slave relationship.

4. Bullies will throw tantrums just to ensure that their importance is validated. Others around will feel the need to placate these bullies at all costs and give in to their unnatural demands just to maintain the peace.

5. Bullies avoid making decisions. They will deflect taking decisions as this will make them accountable. Not making a decision is their escape mechanism. When faced with the outcome later, a bully will always take a high moral ground. He/she will take all credit for the good work and be the first to blame in case things are not showing a positive trend.

6. When asked for their advice or opinions, a classic bully response is to prevaricate. By not giving a clear direction and opinion, they will save themselves and then later align themselves with the winning side and showcase how they are always right.

7. Bullies will hold others responsible and accountable. They have clear directions and guidelines on what others need to do. This will, however, not apply to themselves. They dispense these opinions freely but their actions and behaviours will not match them.

8. They will try to gain your sympathy. They will have multiple scenarios that they will share showing you how others have oppressed them.

9. They will always have at least one enemy at any given point in time, someone who is creating problems for

them. This validates their feeling of always being a victim and having been wronged.

The surprising factor here is that the enemy can keep changing and as a result their friends too keep changing. If A is the enemy, then B and C are friends or well-wishers. But if B becomes the enemy, then C and A will become friends. This is a constant cycle and needs to be accepted by everyone who surrounds the bully. No explanation or opinion works here. If they display empathy towards the bully they are friends but if they try to reason with the bully, they are automatically stigmatised as foes. The best scenario is to stay uninvolved and be indifferent as bullies feed off sympathy too.

Bullies need to realise that no energy will now come their way. It is only when they realise this factor after all their stratagems, that transformation will take place. They need to realise that their regular methods are no longer working. It is difficult to face up to these bullies but the effect is as important as a surgeon's knife. It needs to be done. The process is long as they will increase the intensity of their tantrums before conceding defeat. Sometimes, they will even cut themselves off from you. This is difficult to handle especially when it is someone who is your manager, your family member or someone else close to you. Stay strong and give them that space. Let them stay away. Don't nurture any hard feelings for them. Send positive and loving thoughts. Be the surgeon who needs to stay impassive and positive while being involved. Do your duty to them but don't get involved in their stories and never, ever give up your energy. Bullying is a disease and needs to be nipped in the bud for a healthy, progressive and equalitarian society to grow.

I am not aware whether I have been blessed or cursed but in my lifetime I have had to face up to many bullies. At the start of the book, I mentioned an incident that had taken place in my life. That was a broken engagement. Being Indian, I was okay with the concept of an arranged marriage. My family received a marriage proposal for me when I had just turned 20. We just didn't connect and three months later, just three weeks before the wedding date, my mother took the bull by the horns and called off the wedding. At the time, my father took the high ground, saying that he had been opposed to the engagement in the first place. This was my first inkling of the non-accountable and high-ground behaviour expressed by a bully. I am sorry to say that at the time, I believed him.

When another marriage was arranged for me later, I kept looking to my father for guidance. I repeatedly asked for his opinion. I was waiting for him to take the final call and trusted him to guide me as he had expressed his opinions clearly earlier. Needless to say, I kept waiting. After no input from him, I agreed to the marriage after a discussion with my mother. Later, much later, when I was unhappy in my marriage, my father proclaimed that he had never been happy with the decision in the first place but no one had asked his opinion. My learning regarding a bully's mindset started from here. I learnt that I could not trust my father's words. The association of this behaviour with being a bully came much later.

How are bullies created?

Is someone born a bully? While upbringing can play a role in creating this mentality, it is not the sole reason. Children who had to fight for attention at home may sometimes display these bully-like behaviours during their teenage years. However, a bully can be made anywhere, anytime. Each of us can become a bully. It is a natural phenomenon as this is the easiest form of gaining energy. In management speak, this is called a top-down approach. The flow of power is from the topmost hierarchy to lower levels. It is easy to show your power and dominate others who are dependent on you. In a professional environment, the boss has all the power while on the personal front, the head of the family is the most dominating personality. Why? Because it is very easy to wield power over those who are dependent on us.

Humans are constantly on the lookout for energy. You can easily lord over others who present themselves as easy targets. I remember a saying 'A man's true character can be seen only when he is in power'. This is so true. It is only when someone has power that their true nature seeps out. You will show your power over people who are weaker than you. When others are deferring to you, looking up to you, it is easy to become used to this power. If you are not someone who can generate their own energy, you will easily become used to this easy power and become a dictator in your own world. It takes a strong individual who generates their own energy to refrain from dominating others. To not steal the energy of others around them but instead share his/her energy with others.

This energy-stealing, power-wielding behaviour is not just limited to your boss or someone higher up in the hierarchy. This is the easiest form of energy stealing. Many times in the past I've seen my house help come to work with bruises. She suffered from domestic abuse. Her husband was a drunkard and earned less than her. However, in a patriarchal society, he was convinced that just because he was male, he had the complete right to ill-treat his wife and children.

When handling a team and during stressful situations, I realised I too was prone to losing my temper. I realised the change in the behaviour of my team and family members after such an event.

You don't need to be successful or an achiever or even someone senior at the workplace to show your power. If you are not able to generate your own energy, at one or more times in your lives, you may be guilty of displaying bully-like behaviour. How quickly you realise your mistake and return to normal depends on your inner strength and realisation of your values and identity.

A bully can be someone around you who has gone through a trauma or a relationship problem—a teenager going through hormonal changes, someone suffering through illness or financial crises or issues at work. These circumstances make people short-tempered, vocal, wanting sympathy, becoming selfish, or behaving like someone you need to handle with velvet gloves. *The victim creates the bully.* You begin by excusing their behaviour and giving them space. The bully is created since they get easy sympathy and start gaining power over others. In most cases, this starts a trend for increased bullying and the bully starts feeding off the energy being received so easily.

Over time when this energy is no longer forthcoming, the intensity of their behaviour increases. The higher the intensity, the higher the energy demand. It is this behaviour of people who easily become victims that creates bullies. If not checked, this easy access to energy and acceptance of their bullying by others will eventually turn them into bullies. Once created, bullies will employ the same tactics which were useful earlier and keep increasing their radius to unconsciously convert more targets.

To stop this behaviour, you need to first understand whether, unconsciously, you too are guilty of giving away your energy or nurturing relationships that are creating bullies. You might be giving your energy to someone close to you by excusing their behaviour. But are you ready to face the consequences of the person getting addicted to this free energy and trying to steal from others?

It's important to identify if you are unconsciously giving up your energy or are having your energy stolen. If you are giving up your energy, you will experience any or all of the following symptoms:

1. A lethargy in your body after the encounter. You will feel the need to recharge yourself.
2. You feel your brain is on vacation and you are not able to think.
3. You will feel the need for some time alone.
4. Feel hurt or confused.

5. Feel that energy level is low.
6. You might experience a craving for comfort food or stronger addictive substances.

You know it's a bully when you find yourself trying to explain or excuse their behaviour to others.

You know it's a bully when you find excuses for not standing up to them.

You know it's a bully when your mind does not work. You would normally have come up with ideas or solutions but somehow in this case your brain is just not working.

You know it's a bully when someone is emotionally blackmailing or manipulating you.

You know it's a bully when they want you to conform to their notion of what's best for you.

You know it's a bully when after the encounter, your stress levels are high and you seek relief through food, alcohol or other things.

What is the most effective way to become resilient when faced with bullying?

The purpose is to not just be resilient but to sustain your energy. You must not allow the bully in your life to snatch any energy away and get the bully to steadily and slowly start changing his/her/their behavioural patterns.

I've found that the most effective way to do all this is to be silent. When faced with bullying, take a mental step back and do not show any reaction. The best way for you is to keep calm and keep repeating inside you, "I am calm and in control of my energy. This energy has been generated by me, by my actions, my thoughts, my prayers, etc. I am the guardian of my energy. I am not giving this away."

A word of warning is required here. Such a scenario usually makes the bully more aggressive. It's like training a child. When you want to wean the child away from something, the first reaction is a tantrum. It's similar for a bully when they are being weaned away from their easy access to your energy. They get more and more aggressive. They are not easily placated like children. They will usually try all possible options to intimidate, threaten, and overshadow you or even influence others against you before they can realise the error of their ways.

You need to be strong and think about what is your truth. Are you happy and energised? Over time, there will be a change. While you cannot explain things to the bully during a full-blown tantrum, maybe later, when the time is right, you can softly put forth your point. If you were insulted by the bully, you can explain why what was said by them was insulting, why you do not deserve this and why you need to be respected. You have earned it. If you felt that someone was taking advantage of you, similarly at a later time, you can softly point out that you have thought over what was discussed but felt that this was not suitable for you.

You must stress your message softly so that the bully can listen. You cannot raise red flags in the bully's mind by countering his/her tactics. Wait for some time and softly state your viewpoint. It's a known fact that loud voices make us deaf and to listen to soft voices we need to be more acute and in listening mode. Raise the volume of your television and try to converse with people around you. You will find that loud noises cancel out other voices. Now decrease the sound of the television. Try listening to it. You will automatically find that you need to concentrate more to listen. It is the same with humans. You avoid loud noises and speak softly to be heard. You cannot speak softly during the tantrum. Hence wait your turn and speak when the time is right.

Why do good people suffer?

Have you also felt that this is the case? Someone you know is good but is surrounded by toxic relationships or is undergoing a lot of drama in his/her/their lives. Such people are always victims of circumstances. This is, in part, due to the quality of their energy. They have raised the quality of their energy through their good deeds, prayers, and selfless actions. We will focus on this part in the later section of this book. You can raise your energy levels through certain exercises and this will be covered in detail in volume 2. However, it's important to understand that the energy of certain people is somehow purer than others. I've witnessed this scenario multiple times and have realised that this is quite common. Their energy is more addictive than that of others. Furthermore, with their selfless behaviour, they tend to excuse the behaviour of others around them and are always in a giving mode. They start attracting bullies or they create bullies around them who get addicted to this easily accessible energy.

When you steal from a pure soul, while there is an instant feeling of power, there are consequences. This energy does not last and ebbs away more quickly than normal. This creates some powerful bullies who are always on the hunt for energy. Good people have become bullies because of their proximity to these pure souls. Everyone needs to learn how to sustain their energy and not allow it to be stolen. It's important to remember that the bullies being created here are not strangers. They are close to us and can include our siblings, spouses, children, subordinates, or parents.

Vulnerable moments can cause this energy-stealing trait to emerge. What are these vulnerable moments? A prolonged illness, stress at work, relationship issues, or anything that creates a weakness within can turn a normal individual into a bully. The easy sympathy or the overcompensation they receive from others can create this monster. Once they have access to this power, they repeatedly and unconsciously try to regain the same state.

The energy gained through external sources is temporary. Easy come and easy go. The bully is more scared of losing energy. Losing it makes the bully more moody, aggressive, hungry, demanding and urgent in his/her need for this energy as it can make them powerful again. Awareness about energy is paramount. Only when you are aware can you work on generating your own soul energy without stealing it from others. You also need to sustain it so that others around you cannot get access and become the bullies in your life.

Once you learn to generate your soul energy, you will realise that it is highly liberating. It is different from that derived from physical fitness. This energy will make you happy. You won't need a reason, an achievement or an event. You remain happy, not due to anything specific, you just are.

I have observed that bullies who do not learn to generate their energy and lose their power over others tend to develop major health issues. They could also be trying to gain sympathy from others for their illness and this could be an extension of their earlier energy-gaining process. Whatever the case, it cannot be denied that they do go through some debilitating health issues. They must learn to heal themselves. However, most bullies become so set in their ways that they operate like a see-saw and tend to retry their old ways wherever possible. They will try to use the same methods that got them easy success earlier and made them feel powerful. Like before, this needs to be countered and discouraged.

Just by keeping calm, being peaceful, and not giving up your soul energy, you can check this trait in others and inspire them. For every bully, there will come a time when he/she no longer has anyone to overpower and will feel weak. Their vampire tendencies will create suffering in their lives and may even lead to painful and lonely deaths. Feel sorry for the bullies. Don't give away your energy but do feel sorry for them.

It's also important to note that facing and recognising bullying does not turn you into a bully. You will resist the efforts of others to take away your energy but you are not trying to steal their energy. Be calm, strong, kind, active, positive, and assertive. Be neither passive nor aggressive.

You don't need to become like the bullies yourself. Just be the best you that you can be. It's not easy to be a bully and to always hunt for energy. Start your forgiveness process towards the bullies in your life.

The forgiveness process

When facing the brunt of the bullies in your life, the last thing on your mind will be forgiveness. It's tough. I know. I've been there.

How can you forgive someone who has given you immense pain?

It all boils down to how much weight you need to carry on you. Our world frowns upon obesity. It's unhealthy. What is not ok in the physical sense is unhealthy in the emotional sense too. All the excess weight we lug around has created mental blocks, and burdens and inhibited our capacity to love. However, without realising it, we carry all the burdens from grudges held, failed relationships, guilt, anger, rejections and much more as additional weight.

Forgiveness also covers other areas of your life. It's the key to changing your mindset from victim mode to empowered mode. A victim will always find someone or something to blame for their deficiencies and lack of success. It takes a big heart to forgive, let go and move on. To clear the space within and open up your heart for more love.

Many people swear by the Hawaiian Prayer for forgiveness called "Ho'oponopono" (pronounced HO-oh-Po-no-Po-no). It consists of repeating the four lines given below in a loop:

I'm sorry.

Please forgive me.

I thank you.

I love you.

You think of the person you would like to forgive and repeat these lines.

You might think it odd that you are asking for forgiveness instead of forgiving the bully in your life. Additionally, you are thanking them and affirming your love for them.

I have discussed this prayer in my sessions and I'm always asked why we need to say 'Thank you' and 'I love you'.

Based on my own experience over the years, I've realised that everyone you attract in your life has a part to play in your evolution, be it positive or negative. Whatever their role, you must always remember that while you can learn forgiveness, it is the bully who is taking on the heavier karma or karmic burden. You cannot learn forgiveness unless you have someone to forgive.

You might have seen movies where revenge is the most powerful emotion. Now imagine a scenario where the bully has taken on this persona only for the victim to learn self-respect, self-awareness and forgiveness. I have faced and also forgiven all the bullies in my own life and can attest to the feeling of empowerment and satisfaction this has created within me.

While Ho'oponopono is a powerful prayer, I have come to realise that where there is a lot of pent-up emotion, each bully must be tackled individually. I'm aware there are a lot of forums where they encourage individuals to personally call the people in your life whom you have a dispute with and ask for forgiveness. This individual could very well be the bully in your life and it is their bullying tendencies that created the dispute in the first place.

Hence, I've personally not felt that this is the way to go. I've seen that this method also attracts some ridicule and condescending behaviour from the individual who is being asked for forgiveness. This is due to the difference in the emotional evolution of both individuals. You are asking for forgiveness as part of your own evolution with a desire to free the burdens within. The same sentiment is not shared by the individual you are seeking forgiveness from.

To understand this difference imagine a teacher who desires to repair the relationship with a child in his class. Maybe he was harsh at one time and now seeks forgiveness to unburden his mind. The child cannot be said to have the same maturity level as the teacher. You can just imagine the child gloating about how the teacher has begged for his/her pardon.

When the emotional maturity levels are disparate, forgiveness cannot be sought vocally but at the level of the soul. Imagine another scenario where the teacher approaches the principal or headmaster of the school and lays the matter bare. In the forgiveness process, the principal is the soul of the child or the other individual. Hence forgiveness here works at a soul-to-soul level.

I had the most disparate and stressful relationship with my father, my ex-husband, and two of my ex-bosses. To seek their forgiveness face to face would have been a most uncomfortable experience for me. This method allowed me to beg for forgiveness without speaking to them personally.

Furthermore, it was becoming essential to clear the air with forgiveness as this was affecting my relationship with my son.

To clarify, most of you will have these emotional relationships and these can be traced back to the relationship you have had with either your mother or father. The relationship with your father defines your future relationships with all the men in your life. Similarly, your relationship with your mother defines your relationships with all women in your life.

My unresolved emotional distress with my father had affected my relationship with my husband, now ex, and my ex-bosses and I could see the beginning of this lack of connection with my son as well. It was time to clear the space and forgive all the men in my life.

I've found the best method for seeking this forgiveness is by creating a safe space in your mind. Imagine a mountain top that you can ascend to. Imagine a plateau on the mountain where there are innumerable doors. Behind each door are people whom you have this emotional distress or disparity with. It no longer matters what they or you have done. It's important that you clear the air with each individual through forgiveness. This applies to all the important relationships in your life.

Now visualise you are behind one of these doors facing someone one on one. This is a safe space as you are speaking to the soul of the person and not face-to-face. You speak to them, beg their forgiveness, and do what it takes to put forth your sentiments and clear the burden from your heart and soul. If you feel it's required, at the soul level itself you can visualise touching their feet to show your repentance and desire to clear the air with them.

Now imagine that they are saying, "Yes, I forgive you." You reciprocate by saying, "I forgive you too." You need to do this until you have cleared the space within you. You can direct your love towards them. Acknowledge that they have taken on this heavy karmic burden so that you could learn forgiveness, self-awareness, self-respect or any other quality of God that you were meant to learn for this life. We are going to cover the qualities of God later in this book.

When you step out of this particular door on the mountain, you need to imagine that the door and the room behind you have vanished completely. Similarly, you will approach other doors and see these rooms also disintegrate behind you. These vanishing doors do not signify that the individual has vanished from your life, but actually, you have cleared some degree of the emotional disconnect with them. Initially, you will need to repeat this process daily until you feel a sense of relief within and later you can repeat this once or twice a week.

I have cleared all the emotional discord with all the males and females in my life and now just do a blanket forgiveness ritual daily. I imagine that I am seeking forgiveness from the super soul and this constitutes everyone in my current and past lives. My forgiveness statements are as below:

God, please forgive me if I have hurt anyone in this lifetime or any past life.

I have forgiven everyone completely.

I feel an abundance of love for everyone and this guides all my actions.

You can now also repeat the powerful Ho'oponopono prayer. Once you have cleared the individual discord, this prayer works magically. It releases all your emotions and empowers you with love.

There is one more type of forgiveness that I would like to add here. I believe the forgiveness process cannot be thought to be complete without knowing about the bow-and-arrow effect of forgiveness.

In 2015, I was blessed to attend an event with Dr. Kaity Cama in Mumbai. She is a speaker and healer. During the event, she mentioned forgiving those who had defrauded you. This topic hit me hard. In my family we have seen many major cases of property and financial takeovers, robbing close family members of their rightful share. I have seen the devastation such actions brought within the family and how difficult it is for them to forgive. Especially when the thieves flagrantly displayed their lavish lifestyles. Their actions caused a divide within the family. To forgive them seemed unthinkable

I raised this issue with Dr. Cama and her response gave me a completely new perspective and in the process empowered me. She said that until forgiveness takes place the entire burden of the fraud is shouldered by the victim. The victim in essence is not allowing a lessening of his/her burden by holding onto not just the actual event but also to the emotion generated. The pain from the event creates a victim mindset and this colours all actions in all other areas of life. Hence, as per Dr. Cama, if you have been the recipient of such an action, it's important to let go of the negative emotions.

This letting go is not through being helpless or escapism but through an empowered process. You need to think of the event and the individuals who have perpetuated the event and in your mind say the following line:

"God grant you the strength to bear this karmic burden" and then quietly let the event clear from your mind. A metaphoric letting go.

I remember speaking to her, seeking more clarity. She shared her experience that I'm not repeating here because it's not my story to share.

She inspired me that day and I learnt the power of letting go, by not being a victim but by letting go consciously and letting the universe handle the event. Basically, allowing karma to handle it in its own way.

In India, we are comfortable speaking of karma and the numerous lives we as humans live to sort through all the karma accumulated from our past lives. However, I started realising that this forgiveness mentioned by Dr. Cama has other karmic connotations too. Over time, there were a lot of dots that got connected and the answers revealed themselves.

While this topic is huge and will be covered further as part of 'The Dependability Circle' in volume 2 of the E-volvement series, it's important to cover the money vibration related to frauds perpetuated and its resultant forgiveness.

You might ask how karma gets activated specifically when it comes to money. In the karmic world, money is not a commodity but an energy, a means of achieving and accomplishing all that you have been tasked with for this lifetime. Money is to be used for daily requirements, looking after your family, education, medical expenses, buying or maintaining a home, legal expenses and more.

In the karmic sense, when an economic fraud takes place, it is not just money that is taken. The one forcibly and unethically taking the money is in essence also taking responsibility for the money that is to be spent in the areas defined above. The stealer is also taking over the related burdens for which this money had been designated.

I saw this happen within my family. Until the revenge factor was strong, the stealers kept on enjoying the money without facing the actual karmic burden related to the money. It was only when forgiveness and a letting go of the emotion related to the event was implemented that a chain reaction began, which led to the downfall of the stealers. Since then I have worked with many clients and once we start them on the forgiveness process, they have also witnessed many such occurrences. A special mention: letting go and forgiving done with an aim to teach the other person a lesson does not work.

I now call this the 'Bow and Arrow effect.' Any pain or burden being carried by you for sins done to you is the bow and arrow carried by you. You are always in a state of readiness to find your target and shoot the arrow. The thief is unconcerned with your actions and it is solely your body that is bearing the brunt of this burden.

Furthermore, the arrow in question is double-edged. While you are pointing this outwards, its blade has created a hole within you and does not allow for healing to take place.

For healing to begin, it's important to release the bow and arrow, to set it down, and to free yourself from the karmic burden. It is not your burden to carry. It is only when you set it down that you can release yourself from this karmic burden. When you repeat the line "God grant you the strength to bear this karmic burden," you are not just releasing the burden carried by you but also blessing the thieves. May they have the strength to bear the burden their actions and greed have created for them as they now have to additionally bear the burdens connected to the money stolen by them.

I had a client who had been fighting property-related court cases. She was filled with hate for the tenants who had taken possession of her property. The legal system in India does not allow for speedy justice and she had already faced this for the past 7 to 8 years. We worked on releasing her hate, understanding what she was meant to learn from this occurrence and also forgiving them. Once she cleared her inner angst, the court case too started moving faster and within two years she had regained her property and her life.

A family friend was very hard-working. She lived in a joint family and was responsible for the entire family. An astrologer informed her that this was written in her karma. She was also facing health issues at the time. It so happened that the money due to her husband was stolen by his brother. There was a lot of strife, disintegrating the joint family unit.

I really appreciated her when she continued living her life through forgiveness. I remember having long discussions with her, trying to understand her stance. She readily forgave them. She said, "If I'm meant to have this money, it will find its way back to me." She even convinced her husband to forgive his brother and mend the family ties. What I found interesting was the transformation this wrought in her own life. With the disintegration of the joint family, she became free of all her initial responsibilities. The same astrologer was surprised and said that the lines on her palm had changed. She was now assured that she would have an easy life. And she did. The entire burden of the family was shifted to her brother-in-law. It was not a simple burden either. The money that he had defrauded them of did not cover the years of medical, educational, and household expenses that he faced over the years. This is not counting the added stress from such expenses. My friend, on the other hand, started enjoying better health and freedom.

Forgiveness is the key to handling such negative events and becoming free of burdens. You process the event not through pain but through empowerment and love. This creates the transformation you desire.

A bully versus a strong personality

Are all powerful people bullies? Is everyone around you trying to steal your energy?

In every field, you hear of powerful personalities who cannot tolerate inefficiency. Steve Jobs was said to be one such boss. He was known to be exacting and eccentric. How can you distinguish between a powerful personality and a bully?

If you have been acquainted with one of many powerful personalities, I'm sure this is a question that is going through your mind. On your journey through life, you will meet many powerful and successful individuals. Not all powerful souls are out for your energy. Some have unlimited bundles of energy. They are power-packed personalities that might leave you feeling dazed.

How can you differentiate them from bullies? If I have to provide a visual image, then the bully can be compared to an earthquake that leaves destruction in its wake. The ground itself trembles and you are not sure where you stand. The earthquake will tear up the ground and not allow for any growth. On the other hand, a powerful personality can be compared to the wind. The wind will appear destructive only when faced with a weak structure. Have you ever seen powerful winds blowing and been thankful for the safety of your home? Your home is strong and safe and protects you. With such individuals, cultivating a strong personal presence yourself can shield you. You too have to strive to become an achiever, to keep learning, to keep growing, and to earn their respect.

Such is the magnificence of these powerful individuals. They have a powerful presence and their personality is power packed. They are super achievers. They know what they want and have built their momentum over the years. They race ahead in their quest to achieve their goals, vision and mission. They do not plan to bring about anyone's downfall but their momentum can daze or destroy other weaker souls. Not every structure can stand in the path of the gusty winds and survive. Their sheer energy and pace are dismaying to most.

What traits characterise these wind souls i.e. souls of people with powerful personalities?

- They are negligent in following the social hierarchy and only appreciate the ones they respect
- They respect very few people
- They will expect more from you than you ever dreamed possible
- They are constantly pushing, challenging, and aggravating others around them just to get reactions and create more capacity within them
- There will always be several complaints against them in social scenarios
- They are quick to give feedback
- They are young know-it-alls and will almost always be young achievers
- They will not be happy in the traditional or tried and tested businesses

- Their businesses will be modern, new age and bring about massive change in their area of focus
- They are happy when you grow or defy them
- They delight in your success
- They appreciate strong personalities around them
- They appreciate your expertise in your field
- They surround themselves with experts from different streams
- They are always hungry to learn and know more
- Their sense of humour and liking for certain subjects will not be understood easily by others
- They can be perceived as dictators, however, they are benevolent and not destructive

Here are some indications that you have encountered a strong personality.

- You are intimidated by their pace, their knowledge and their sheer energy
- You feel they do not accord you the respect that you deserve
- You have to earn their respect consistently
- You need to constantly keep up with them
- You feel stretched mentally every time you meet them
- Keeping up with them ensures that you start achieving more than you ever dreamed possible

- The minute you feel weak, they will steamroll you or so it may seem

How is the bully different? The bully will consciously or subconsciously not allow others to grow. The methods employed by the powerful individuals might be unusual and unorthodox but the intention behind them is to encourage, challenge, stretch and grow those whom they respect and those who can stand up to them.

If you are blessed enough to have powerful individuals in your life, stop complaining. Try finding ways to make yourself better. Ask for their help. Take their feedback constructively. Be prepared to receive more feedback than you are comfortable with. Be grateful for such people. Become worthy of having such a person in your life. Continue adding value to yourself and your productivity when around them. If you let them, these individuals will carry you on the strength of their vision, and you will achieve much more than you ever dreamed possible.

You can all be perceived as sources of light. Your soul energy lights up your own Gami-Verse. Your bulb allows the light to shine through. However, some bulbs will shine much brighter than others due to the sheer strength of their personality and will cause others in their surroundings to shine brighter too. While you all may desire soul energy, some will compete against others or even resort to stealing it through bullying. Others will stay weak their entire life and continue to blame others.

What is the most obvious sign of low soul energy: assigning blame to others and not taking responsibility for their failures. However, many other scenarios and circumstances deplete your soul energy.

All of us are born with pure souls. You need to only hear a child gurgling to feel the purity of their soul. You are all born with full cups of energy. These get depleted as time goes by and this depends on what or whom we come in contact with.

As shared earlier, each one of you carries your energy or Gami-Verse around with you. The weaker the energy, the more prone you are to take on the characteristics of others who surround you. These may be individuals whom we perceive as being stronger than us. You are always looking outside for the key to your happiness. You may want to imitate successful people so that, in some unknown manner, their success will rub off on you.

This seeking of energy from those around them is the reason why so many people imitate others and try to speak or appear like others. You may take on fake accents, wear branded clothes that you cannot afford, and stay visible in venues that will make you famous by association. It's the same as living a lie. This is a major reason that depletes energy. The more you try to emulate others to show them how perfect you are, the more your energy gets depleted.

Sadly, this is the age of perfectionism. Everyone aims for a perfect lifestyle by looking and seeming perfect. People discard 100 pics before posting that one perfect image on social media. You not only want to show what you are like but also want to gain acceptance and acknowledgement for your perfectionism.

I'm as guilty of this as everyone else. I wanted to help others but when I adopted social media, I had to overcome my insecurity of appearing less than perfect. I realised that I could only aim to look my best. I cannot aim to look as perfect as celebrities. Celebrities are paid for the way they appear. This external validation causes all the unhappiness. I knew someone who suffered from vitiligo. She gave up the pretence of looking perfect years ago. She now looks the best she can.

The more you look outside for happiness, the more you take on the characteristics of others around you. You may see their positives but are unaware of what they suffer deep inside. Everyone has their own internal goals to achieve, and their limiting beliefs to overcome. By associating with their superficial persona, you also tend to take on their negatives. You might admire a celebrity but are you aware of what they are going through? Find out who you are and be the best that you can be.

Are you aware that your flaws will create more connections for you as compared to your perfections? The most long-lasting connections are made when you show your flaws and reveal your weaknesses. They showcase your human side. You appear more real to others and hence you connect better. Don't take this literally and post pictures on social media with you digging your nose. That is the other extreme. I am just saying that don't deplete your energy by always trying to be perfect. When connecting with others, either on a one-on-one or one-to-many basis, be comfortable. Make your flaws your biggest strengths. Share your story, showcase your human side, and laugh at yourself. For instance, Jennifer Lawrence gives the best interviews. She's not afraid of showing her human side. You don't need to imitate anyone, just find your most comfortable persona and create your style.

Other limiting beliefs that deplete your energy

The beliefs of everyone around you while growing up play a major role in your energy depletion. You absorb these negative beliefs and they cloud your universe. You are no longer living under the open sky, like when you were born, but are burdened by all the dark clouds of your upbringing.

Here are some of the general limiting beliefs I see around me:

- Brahmins are not open to change
- Punjabis are alcoholics and only want fun in their lives

- Muslims have violent tendencies because they do halal
- Christians are missionaries and will want to convert you
- Women cannot drive
- Women cannot manage money
- Aged relatives are boring
- Alcohol is fun. If you don't drink, you are boring
- Boys don't cry
- Grown-up boys cannot hug their mothers or sisters
- If you've got it, flaunt it

And wait for it, my personal favourite:

- Women are the doorway to hell

This was probably said by someone who had weak soul energy and could not control his impulses. Hence he created this belief not just to excuse his behaviour but to provide an excuse to the world at large for their weaknesses. You may ascribe to these or other limiting beliefs while trying to make sense of the world around you. By the time you realise these are limiting beliefs, you have spent a good amount of time living them. Overcoming them becomes your challenge for this lifetime. These negative beliefs make you think from a place in your past and hence many people today live their life in the past. They cannot accept change or adapt to new inputs. Their universe is bogged down with these limiting beliefs. They have clouded their universe and they see through these brown-coloured spectacles.

How can you identify people who are living in the past?

Such people will have a lot of opinions. How can they not? They have a museum full of artefacts within their universe to refer to. As inside, so is it outside. You can check their homes. They would have surrounded themselves with a lot of collectables. They are not hoarders who are clinging to things but individuals whose homes resemble museums. Your home is an extension of your inner identity. Just by viewing someone's home, you can understand their beliefs. They will also be opinionated and freely dispense advice. They will take time to make decisions and will need to first verify all the facts, cross all the T's and dot all the I's before coming to a decision.

Living in the past is the opposite of living in the future. I always imagined that it would be impossible to live in the future until I realised I was guilty of this. I too tend to live in the future. Others like me who have had a traumatic experience think similarly. Everyone who has gone through trauma will want to gloss over the present and live in the future.

Anyone around you who is talking fast and has big goals but has little or no clue how to achieve them is living in the future. Their ability to not focus on the present is directly proportional to the level of trauma they have experienced. Oddly enough, you might find such individuals normal. Their behaviour would not reflect the trauma hidden within them. They have glossed over and escaped the trauma that is in their present and conveniently escaped to a point in their future by making plans. Once they start clearing the traumatic areas of their life, their awareness of their present increases. I can attest to this personally.

I have faced some traumatic events in my past, related to health issues and bullying. My life till now has been a giant project to overcome these issues. My escapist tendencies from my teenage years have settled down and I no longer try to fast forward my present. If I'm asked to state what living in the future seems like then it's like a mental and emotional switch has been turned off or certain events of the past have been edited out of the movie of my life. Similarly, you don't realise it but editing these out makes you jump forward. This is like a movie in the editing phase, where certain sections are removed. As a result, there are gaps in the storyline. Some things don't make sense. It's the same case with people living in the future. In your conversation with them, there are gaps. Their actions and words do not always match.

These cases have to be handled with a lot of care. Everyone has their way of coping with the trauma in their life. Your coping mechanisms are nothing but your attempts to make sense of all the events that have transpired within your life and how they have transformed your universe.

Types of coping mechanisms

The eggshell mechanism

This mechanism is exactly like its name. The eggshell is hard on the outside but fragile, soft and vulnerable on the inside. Souls that have been hurt very often create a hard barrier around them. They are scared of letting anybody within their Gami-Verse lest it create more hurt. They withdraw inside this seemingly impenetrable barrier but are vulnerable just the same. Such people are very fragile and need to be handled with care. During coaching, I've come across many of them. They are aware that they are hurt but cannot let it go since they have to accept it first and relive it, something they would rather not do. Imagine a room within your home that contains all the garbage while the rest of the home is nice and squeaky clean. The garbage tends to collect, and unless addressed, will explode one day.

While coaching such individuals, I've found that the sessions can take dramatic turns. What starts as a seemingly innocuous story or statement can lead to a big volcano waiting to explode. These individuals need to be handled with care—with velvet gloves and a lot of love. However, once they start healing, they will actively seek you out and their true self will start shining through. They want to be healed but just don't know the way.

The hoarder mechanism

Fear and insecurity give rise to a hoarder mentality. Real-life hoarders operate in a state of scarcity. What starts as a means of ensuring everything is available to them when required, creates a situation of excess and they find comfort in it. The same is the case for low-energy souls who start identifying with others. They find peace while dealing with others' problems, are vocal about what is happening around them, and hoard emotions that probably don't belong to them. They are full of opinions on matters unrelated to them and are always competing with others even when it is unnecessary.

The hoarder mechanism prompts them to hold on to their opinions and proclaim them as the ultimate truth. They are comfortable with their version of the truth. In some cases, there may be some truth in their version of events, but they do not acknowledge things that take place after the initial trauma. It is as if their internal software does not get an update. If you find someone talking vehemently of years gone by and defending their opinions loudly to the exclusion of everything else, the person has most likely undergone severe trauma that has affected them to their core.

A self-satisfied and high-energy soul will not be a victim of FOMO (Fear of Missing Out). If you know anyone who has a vociferous need to share their opinion and tries to deflect from his/her internal self and starts hoarding, you are probably face to face with someone who is coping in this way. This is the way such people deal with trauma. These hoarders may also have homes that are overfilled with artefacts and closets filled with clothes. As you are inside, so you are outside. If the hoarding gets severe, they may attract severe and, in some cases, even terminal illnesses. These hoarders are very difficult to coach. They cannot accept any new inputs. It's only when they reach out that you can start their healing process.

Many family members reach out to me to coach hoarders in their families. I've always refused. I believe that for coaching and healing to take place, the person who needs it has to reach out, it cannot be imposed upon them. Of the few that I have coached, the ones who reached out—well, they didn't want to evolve completely. They want to heal but have set boundaries. Once they get relief from their immediate and pressing concerns, they retreat into their zone of comfort. They don't want to be completely healed and become free from all encumbrances.

The cactus mechanism

Certain beliefs and events have caused some people to present with a prickly exterior that is similar to a cactus. A 'Do Not Touch' sign has been put up. Approach at your own risk. The cactus mechanism is usually related to just a few random events that have created a distance which has now become involuntary. These individuals no longer know how to connect to others. They desire the company of others but are unable to reach beyond this self-erected barrier.

Just as the thorns of the cactus deflect proximity, the internal cactus within you discourages others from coming closer. What probably started as a simple emotion of wanting to be comfortable and not going beyond your comfort zone has created a cactus-like situation. Such people are happy being left alone. But they may suddenly realise that the world has accepted their narrative and has happily moved away.

This is more common in individuals who are introverts. Extroverts derive their energy from social interaction. Introverts need time alone to recoup their energy. As they already have limited interactions with people, they are more susceptible to the cactus mode. When in need, they are unable to reach out and will retract behind a prickly exterior.

Coaching has worked wonders for people who follow the cactus mechanism of coping. As the soul energy grows, the ability to connect also grows. Their ability to reach out to others and to let others in rises exponentially. Business owners who are in this mode achieve the ability to network and collaborate and this is reflected in the success that many have achieved later. Support groups where everyone is battling similar issues are a major step in the right direction. No one steals energy and everyone applauds each milestone. Furthermore, the human connection with like-minded souls is a strong energy booster. Journalling also helps such people.

The bully mechanism

The bully is always looking for easy targets from whom he/she can steal energy. Bullies do not take any responsibility for their actions but blame others. They are never angry, it's you who have made them angry. They are peaceful, it's you who incited them to violence. This aspect has been covered in the earlier section and is the main reason why the world is suffering today. Too many people have adopted the bully mechanism to survive. For the world to evolve, bullies need to accept responsibility for their actions and not blame others, and also for people to stop the bullies from stealing their energy. It's not the bullies who create victims but victims who create the bullies.

While coaching, it is sometimes tough to spot a bully. Their inner narrative doesn't bring up their bullying mentality. They resort to coaching as a last resort. The bullies that I have coached came to me when they had already alienated one or many close people. Furthermore, they appeared clueless about why others were bullying them. It's important to identify whether the alienated relationships have been caused by others who are bullies or by individuals who have had enough and are now retaliating. Bullies are also adept at portraying themselves as victims. Their mental narrative is that it's not their fault.

The trick to identifying bullies is to observe their facial expressions when they talk about their failed relationships. You will glimpse anger with harsh features distorting their face, especially when they talk about certain people. That's the catch. It's important for them to start creating their soul energy themselves and to learn about how they are destroying others by stealing their energy. I've had some amazing breakthroughs with some bullies that I've coached.

I remember one client who had been guilty of adopting the bullying mentality right from her childhood. She had been developing steadily into a dominant personality that made her blame others from a young age onwards. During a particular session where we revisited her childhood, the session spiralled as she was flooded with guilt due to her actions in her childhood. It took us two hours to clear her baggage. This had to be done at the source so as to not let the residue of her past colour her current relationships. This unconscious build-up of guilt within her had been clouding all her present relationships. She dominated others but unknowingly accepted that others had the right to hurt her. While her healing took place over the next few months, this session saw a 50% drop in her anger levels.

The victim mechanism

Have you met people who are always victims? They are always moaning about how others have taken advantage of them. They are always blameless and are having a most god-awful time. They are always in the wrong place at the wrong time. They claim that they are innocent and the world just keeps taking advantage of them.

They are the silent bullies. They are playing on the sympathy card to steal your energy. They alternate between playing the victim, getting you hooked by playing on your sympathy, and then trapping you in their web of silent bullying. You can recognise outright bullying but the victim mechanism can catch you unawares. If someone is always suffering, beware. There would be a reason for this. Why are they attracting so much suffering? It's best to keep a little distance from the perennial victim.

When coaching such people, spiritual practices have worked wonders. Their inner narrative has to be changed completely. Once they start being accountable for their actions, they realise how destructive blaming others is.

Victims would also have toxic relationships from which it is difficult to extricate them. They cannot look at a forceful exit but by regularly increasing their energy, they can reach a level of certainty about their present state. This has been covered later under 3Cs. This elevated sense of self and feeling of accountability creates the change that they desire.

I mentioned my house help in an earlier chapter. She was using the victim mechanism to make sense of the abusive world she lived in. Gently, over time, through a lot of discussions, she was able to raise her soul energy. She realised her self-worth and has since redefined her family dynamics. She is now the emotional support for her family and commands respect not just from her now peaceful husband but also from her extended family.

The associative mechanism

Not everyone employs a bullying or a victim mechanism. Others belong to a certain section of society or a certain community that others might find abnormal. What does this coping mechanism achieve? Weak souls who neither want to bully others nor to be perennial victims get drawn into the collective larger community. They look for a stronger person, leader, team, community, gang, terror organisation, or any other collective with which they can align themselves. A lack of personal identity makes them seek out other powerful energies. They try to become powerful by association.

Choosing this coping mechanism further restricts their ability to make choices as they are now made for them. These are individuals who choose to stay in toxic marriages, join certain communities, agree to the commands of the leader, and allow themselves to be bullied. They associate with those who, according to them, give them power. They do not realise that the stronger universe will completely absorb their weak version. What does this coping mechanism do? It creates a sense of superiority or arrogance within the individual's feeble mind. This is downloaded from the strong leader he/she follows and inhibits his/her growth. Such people see themselves through the lens of the leader and cannot see themselves as individuals.

The 3Cs work well here too. You may get drawn into such toxicity because of low soul energy. Increasing your energy starts the healing process from within. As soul energy rises, your own identity gains ground and you are no longer happy with the earlier status quo of giving up your power to others.

The addict mechanism

This is the most challenging coping mechanism of all. When faced with a stressful day or event, you are all drawn to comfort foods and need a temporary escape. The coping mechanism involving addiction refers to something that is not a temporary escape but is a long-drawn, deep-rooted acceptance of defeat. Such individuals want an escape route. They do not want to play either the victim or the bully; they just want out. This type of individual will need a lot of soul power to change their energy state. For change to happen, they will first evolve to one of the other coping mechanisms and then aim to reach higher soul energy.

What is the definition of addiction? As per the American Society of Addiction Medicine, 'Addiction is a treatable, chronic medical disease involving complex interactions among brain circuits, genetics, the environment, and an individual's life experiences. People with addiction use substances or engage in behaviours that become compulsive and often continue despite harmful consequences.'

An addiction can be for anything. Apart from the big four such as drugs, drinks, cigarettes and sex, addiction can also encompass coffee, tea, television and movies, mobiles, shopping, window shopping, eating, partying, selfies, social media, obsessive-compulsive behaviour (OCD; this behaviour can even involve talking to your mirror image or inanimate objects and being obsessive about the care of inanimate objects) and lots more.

If this kind of behaviour is occasional then it is normal but if it is obsessive then comes under the header of addiction. Addiction is the symptom and not the cause. The cause for addiction is related to traumatic events of the past and needs to be identified on a person-to-person basis. You're suddenly drinking eight cups of coffee to cope with a stressful day. Or binge-watching a series on OTT when you know you have projects due. You know that this behaviour is not normal. This temporary addiction could result from being forced to do a job that is out of your comfort zone, being overwhelmed by tasks outside your present capabilities, or it could be a more deep-rooted addiction because it clashes with your values. For example, a salesperson who is required to sell products he/she believes are harmful or giving in to peer pressure and doing activities that conflict with their moral compass. Others may need to adapt excessively and change their inner narrative to please their spouse or parent. It could also be a child who is not able to express his/her feelings and make decisions because of dominant parental behaviour. There can be many reasons.

Addicts and their family members need to understand the cause. In case someone talks to himself or lives in a fantasy world, it's important to understand what has made them scared to live their life. What are they not facing? In case it is past trauma, its effect must be released. Once they understand the cause, it is easy for people with mild addiction to slowly overcome their behaviour and replace the old trauma-causing inner voice with positive mental vibes.

Example A: Fear of losing money is a natural fear. When creating the replacement, instead of repeating I have money, the narrative can talk about the highest good. The mantra that can be used could be 'My money benefits society and I lead a luxurious life.'

Example B: Fear of falling can be replaced by repeating 'I have excellent balance and lead an active life.'

Louise Hay has an excellent body of work on the best mantras. You can refer to her books 'You Can Heal Your Life' and 'All Is Well' for some amazing mantras created to heal health issues.

Part 3

What needs to change

CHAPTER

04

What happens when energy levels are high?

Then Jesus said, "Father, forgive them; for they know not what they do." This line from the Bible has always fascinated me. Jesus was being crucified. He was being humiliated and sneered at. He had to carry the cross and was crucified next to criminals. I cannot even begin to imagine the levels of soul energy present in Him. In Sikhism, the faith I follow, there have been many martyrs who have stood up for religion. Our fifth Guru was made to sit daily on a burning plate with hot sand poured over him until his death. Our ninth Guru was beheaded for not converting to Islam by the Mughal Emperor Aurangzeb. There are countless others whose stories are just as inspiring.

What kind of soul energy did these individuals have? The kind that gives them the ability to absorb the shocks that life gives. The kind that shows their superhuman capacity. Jesus, like the Sikh Gurus, was a messenger of God. However, what about others?

If humans could display such impassivity and such resilience, then where do we get this from? Is it possible for you to display this too, albeit in a minuscule capacity? High soul energy helps you absorb life's many shocks and disappointments, protects you from the elements, and protects you against the raging storm outside much like a strong home. It is the love and support of your near and dear ones that enables you to be more resilient. It is the energy present in the inner core that stops you from reacting to the smallest impetus and makes you understand the larger picture. That doesn't make you just an observer of life but a participant. It gives you a starring role in your own evolvement.

Is it possible for you as mere humans to get this high energy and feel its presence and support around you? Can it protect you, support you, and provide a loving atmosphere that guides you and shows you the path?

What is high energy?

This high energy is not related to physical energy or having a highly active lifestyle. As shared earlier, please do not confuse the high energy of the athlete with the energy being discussed here. Do not mistake the high prowess shown by athletes on their turf with the high soul energy of humans.

Physical fitness releases dopamine and benefits the mental health of an individual. However, these are not the only criteria for having high soul energy. If this were the case, athletes and physically fit individuals would not suffer from any kind of emotional and mental distress.

I was blessed to have a spiritually-aware mother. I have grown up reading about my Gurus, Yogis and other spiritually-aware souls. There were many interactions with Saints who either visited our home or whom we travelled to meet. I feel truly blessed for the experiences and blessings that were showered on me just because of my connection to my mother and *nani* (maternal grandmother). They were the beacons that lit the way for me.

When I looked back at the story I shared earlier about my broken engagement and the gentle explanation proffered by Joshi Veerji, it made me realise the different levels that you can aspire to. In April 2023, I wrote a blog entitled 'Are you a leader?' available at https://vriin.com/work-dynamics/leadership/are-you-a-leader/. The blog mentioned the three main qualities that define a leader:

- Earthquake proof
- Noise proof
- Future ready

Being noise proof enables you to rise above the noise around you and stay focused on what is important. Being future ready is the ultimate aim. It enables you to plan for all contingencies and not be in a reactive mode. However, the concept of being earthquake proof fascinates and inspires me. It refers to the quality of not letting any event happening to you or around you affect your inner equilibrium. To stay connected to your core. To be resilient. To stand up quickly after this personal earthquake. To not cry in vain for what has happened but to reassure yourself and focus on what needs to be done now. This is the actual starting point from where you can measure your soul energy. When this energy starts rising within you, you will discover an innate calmness. This calmness will enable you to see the good in each situation or to focus on what is next.

That is not to say that once you attain it, you will be able to retain this high energy. You are all ordinary humans and not messengers of God. Soul energy levels are prone to oscillate like a pendulum, there isn't going to be a perennial high or a perennial low. There will always be an oscillation even at high energy levels. However, there will be more highs than lows. The more soul energy you gain, the more enveloped you will be in this protective atmosphere. You will feel the blessings, the love, and the care from the bountiful universe. Even negative events start bringing with them huge learnings and the essence of how everything is connected to the overall picture.

I recall what Joshi Veerji told my mom, "It's been two weeks and you're still upset?" It was unfathomable to him how my mother, who is a spiritual being, could still be attached to the hurt even after two weeks. How was she not able to overcome this? This was my starting point towards understanding this high soul energy that makes you resilient. It stops you from being in the eye of the storm, even if you are at the receiving end of hurt that is making you a victim. It lets you gain control over your own life. It makes you stand up quickly after an event, allows you to see the larger picture, and makes you buoyant even when others around you continue to struggle. It gives you the ability to take a step back and not get sucked into the dramas playing around you. It makes you see the light within even when others are swimming in the darkness.

You will never receive this power from outside. As humans, you are constantly seeking power from others. You believe that there is a magic potion or a heavenly gift that will descend on you and make you strong. The magic is inside each one of you. You are all capable of becoming highly evolved beings. You can understand and evolve from ordinary humans to God-like beings who are in charge of their destiny. You need not be at the mercy of all the elements but can create your path.

The times have changed. There are many more options available in the world today as compared to even 200 years ago. Life is becoming easy on the outside. You no longer need to struggle to accomplish basic everyday tasks. Everything is available at the click of a button. The outside is evolving quickly and the changes you are witnessing would have seemed magical even 15 to 20 years ago. While the outside has changed tremendously, the inside is still struggling. You now need to bring your focus back to the inside.

As humans, you have totally ignored the inside. You have become addicted to the outside and buried what's within you. You no longer belong to the generation of your parents and grandparents who were more satisfied and content with less comfort and more struggle. The world today is fascinated with movies about superpowers and magic. You may long for these extra powers that will help you escape the mundane and find success through external means. However, please realise, there is no magical potion outside of you or being gifted to you that is going to make you happy. Nothing will happen unless you choose to bring your focus back inside and start generating energy. Without this inner soul energy, you are equal to a discharged light bulb. Look around you and you will see a lot of such people. How can you identify them? Their complaints will be the loudest. They are never satisfied and are always looking for the next high, the next thrill and the next escape that will make them forget the struggles in their lives.

A glowing soul that is highly charged can be distinguished among the crowd. Such people will have a quiet assurance about them. You may not spot them easily but you can see the difference their presence brings to their surroundings. They are positive, assured and have self-belief. They encourage others and ensure credit is given where it's due. You will find these special individuals going about their work silently while blissfully displaying their inner contentment. They are loving souls and live as per their code and not as per the sanctions imposed by their surroundings. The higher the charge, the more unique they are.

In the book by Adam Grant entitled 'Give and Take,' he talks of Liz Wiseman who distinguishes between geniuses and genius makers. "Geniuses tend to be takers: to promote their own interests, they 'drain intelligence, energy, and capability' from others. Genius makers tend to be givers: they use their 'intelligence to amplify the smarts and capabilities' of other people, such that 'light bulbs go off over people's heads, ideas flow, and problems get solved.'"

To be a giver requires great soul energy. In a world where everyone is stealing energy to just survive, genius makers are givers who are content to take a backseat. They know that they do not need to steal from others and that the collective win is more important than the individual one. They are on the evolvement path themselves and are helping others evolve too.

Evolvement can happen in multiple areas. You can evolve in your craft, in your talent and skill, in your role within your company, in your role as a parent, a friend, and a confidante. There is no end to evolvement. The trick here is to be continuously on the road to evolvement, to not get stuck in any area, to always see the path ahead, and to be able to move ahead quickly after a disaster or life-transforming event. This can only happen when soul energy levels are high.

Another area that distinguishes a higher soul energy individual from a low soul energy counterpart is faster decision-making ability. Such individuals have an innate belief in God and in the protection they receive from God. I know in today's world speaking of God is considered taboo. The word God is being replaced with vibration or receiving energy from the universe. However, just ignoring or deflecting from the word does not mean God does not exist.

What kind of world are you creating where you deny the rights of its maker? You associate all evils in the world with God and take credit for all that is good. You credit God with one day in the week. Christians associate God with the Sabbath (Sunday), Muslims say Jumma (Friday), and Hindus say Guruvaar or Guru Ka Vaar (Thursday). However, to whom are the other days attributed? You enjoy the creations but have chosen to forget their creator.

Just because you cannot see something does not mean it does not exist. You cannot see the wind but can feel it. You cannot see the atom with your naked eyes but have witnessed its power. The multitude has never seen the atom.

You take the assurance of those who you perceive as being more educated to convince yourselves that the atom exists.

Why then is God being denied? You have had countless men and women of God through the ages telling us about the power, the presence and the blessings of having God in their lives. Every community or tribe around the world has acknowledged the presence of God. Their definitions might change but the concept is universal. The older the civilisation, the more God-centric it is. Over the ages, there have been countless souls who have travelled the path as seekers of God, wishing for God to be revealed to them.

I've been fortunate to be born in India, where there have been many saints and enlightened souls. It is in the company of these saintly souls that I too have received the answers to all my questions. Slowly, I have arrived at my definition of God and acknowledge God's presence in my own life. With all the support I have received over the years, I have challenged society's concept of God and also the explanations received from books and by listening. You either believe in God or you don't, there cannot be a middle path. You cannot be a fence sitter.

With this book, I would like to share my understanding of God and a few of my experiences, hoping these will take you towards a deeper understanding and will support you as you evolve. You have evolved as humans, truth seekers, scientists and seekers of comfort in life. Similarly, it is time to evolve your mind with the concept of God and to seek your truth. I will clarify this in a later section.

You receive your higher energy from God by following certain practices. I have seen first-hand the difference that high soul energy can make and it has made me a believer. I was born a believer but fell off the bandwagon multiple times. I have been guided sometimes gently and sometimes harshly back to my true path. I have seen and lived on both sides and I believe this makes me the ideal person to communicate this.

I will come to that later. Before that, it is important to understand what changes when your soul energy is high. When it is high, you gain the ability to handle more pressure. From getting upset at the smallest things and trying to blame others, you gain an inner strength that makes you responsible for your own life. It makes you accountable. It places you at the active instead of the reactive end. When faced with any negative event, you don't get sucked into the 'Why' of things. Why me? Why am I suffering? What have I done? Instead, there is self-belief. You now say, "What now? What can I do now? Is this important? Can I let it go?"

Hoarding and holding on to emotions is a coping strategy for low-energy souls, whereas high-energy souls let go of all unimportant things. This is not escapism, but a clearing of space. High soul energy individuals do not carry extra baggage with them as they realise that it will only hold them back. They don't watch the news and get angry at what the world is coming to. They instead plan about what can be done to make the world a better place. Such individuals can easily make the shift from poverty to a prosperity mindset. Hence, they have more control over their life. The higher your soul energy, the more attuned you are to your inner voice.

Many of the high soul energy individuals I've interacted with have also shared something interesting, which is common across many of them. They believe they have reduced memory capacity. When reminded, they are able to recollect past events but overall their recall of the past and all it contains shows a marked decrease.

I even had someone close to me enquire if she had now become dull. In my interactions with her, I found that she was as wise as ever. We discussed this detail and I realised that her past has become an empty slate for her. She didn't need to practice mindfulness and living in the present because her past was wiped clean. She still recalls past events but they no longer hold any emotional connection for her and hence are as unimportant as a movie she may have watched a decade ago.

Somebody else I know who has high soul energy mentioned that he struggles to find the right word sometimes. In the past, this person had amazing communication skills and could enthral the crowd with his wisdom. In the flow of the moment, he still retains his superior communication skills but also experiences a blankness within when he is alone. He states that he is happy being alone and experiences a thoughtless state of mind.

The past exists only as an event with no emotional attachment. You only remember events when there is a corresponding emotional association. You will remember feeling hurt, despair, and anger only when this has touched you at an emotional level. Once the emotional connection is removed, the same event will appear like a scene on television. You are involved but not a participant. For high soul energy individuals, their focus has been shifted from being participants to viewers.

Finding God will mean the funeral of all sorrows.

- Sri Yukteshwar from Autobiography of a Yogi.

This does not mean that sorrow will cease to exist. It just means you have understood the part that the universe wants you to play. From someone who blames everyone, you have upgraded to a doer. Your inner voice is now guiding you. You start finding your answers. Not just seeking like the entire world but seeking and finding answers. What does this lead to? Better decision making.

Have you seen a child throwing a tantrum? When it is your child and this happens in a public place, it embarrasses and frustrates you. However, there is a sense of acceptance. The child does not know what he or she is doing. He/she has to be gently but firmly guided towards what is right. A higher soul energy individual understands this difference. They know that most people with low energy are throwing tantrums to attract attention from others. This is their source of energy and they extract the energy they need by seeking attention, sympathy, or through subjugation.

When you have high energy, you realise the need to maintain it and do not allow any marauder to have easy access to what you have created. Blaming others will deplete this energy whereas taking charge will increase it. When faced with failure, what action or reaction will you exhibit? Are you going to let the failure guide you, make you stronger, learn from this challenge and treat it like a stepping stone?

Or will you treat it as the end of all your dreams? Will you stand at the graveside of your failure crying your heart out?

I was impressed by the book 'Who Moved My Cheese?' by Dr. Spencer Johnson. I highly recommend it to everyone. The entire concept of moving on has been conveyed in such a simple way. My mentor, Ron Malhotra, who is an author and speaker, often says, "A professional will take something simple and make it complex. However, an expert will take something complex and make it simple." Through the simplicity of Dr. Johnson's book, you can see the unerring hand of an expert.

The world is constantly changing. Yes, there was an earthquake. Do you continue to stand next to the crevice that opened up in the ground or do you find a safe space? The quicker your decision-making ability, the faster your reality will change. The current world with low-energy souls has associated energy with places and not with people. There is an overwhelming desire to keep places and territories in your control. They prefer keeping things the way they were. Low energy keeps you constantly in a state of fighting and wanting to go back to what was familiar.

Times are changing. There were conquerors in earlier ages with a desire to acquire and rule over more and more land. Then stronger rulers took over. Each period has a cycle. What has started, has to end. You have to decide your reality. You can choose to keep fighting till you die, even though the event has taken place several decades ago or choose to accept the change and move on. Individuals with high soul energy will take the step to rise from failures. They will accept the lesson that the failure has taught them. They also do not associate themselves with failures. They are the souls who travel a new path. They accordingly find the best path and make way for others. These path-breakers are always going to be ridiculed by others with lesser understanding. This doesn't make them failures. Their high energy makes them more determined than usual.

I remember seeing a Hindi movie 'Manjhi' about a man who broke down a mountain to make a road. People laughed at him when he began but where are they now? Nowhere. The movie was based on a true story and the main character derived his energy from his cause. The world will never remember the naysayers. Have you read any book about someone who said No? No such book exists. It's because there is no space dedicated to these people. It is only the ones who rebel and fight against the tide and succeed that are remembered.

No matter how many failures take place, it is the success at the end that rewrites history. How can you withstand failures? You can be associated with a cause and believe in something despite all the odds without listening to all the negatives around you. Is it that simple? No. It's not. However, it's a choice you make to generate soul energy for yourself and keep replenishing it daily.

Since I have experienced both low and high energy, I know which one I will choose. I will pick the latter as it offers me resilience and makes me kind, loving, generous, peaceful, joyous, and compassionate.

High soul energy creates a sense of happiness. According to Mihaly Csikszentmihalyi in his book 'Flow', "What I discovered was that happiness is not something that happens.

It is not the result of good fortune or random chance. It is not something that money can buy or power command. It does not depend on outside events, but, rather, on how we interpret them."

So High energy = Happiness, and

Happiness = Having the best ideas, being in a state of flow, achieving tasks in a fraction of the time otherwise taken, feeling peaceful and contented, viewing the world as heaven, and feeling blessed.

I have constantly worked on generating my soul energy and have experienced the power of high soul energy. I have had the best ideas when my soul energy was high. The amount of quality work I could accomplish in a short period was phenomenal. I remember one occasion where I had been struggling at work with a particular task. I needed to prepare a first draft for a new policy that we wanted to implement. I had done my homework and had jotted down all the areas to be covered. I had even started working on this draft a couple of times but couldn't get beyond the first paragraph.

I realised that my stress was decreasing my energy. I increased my meditation, started clearing my mind and slowing down my thoughts. The mind is an excellent tool but can race faster than a Ferrari if you let it. It works best if you don't allow it to overcome you. My meditation and slowing of the mind worked wonders. Where I had been struggling earlier, I was able to draft a 4-page policy document in just three hours. This is the power of your mind when your soul energy levels are high.

There is a story my mother told me as a child. A man had been praying to his Guru for years. His Guru was happy with his prayers and granted him a boon. He gifted him a genie to carry out all his work. The man could ask this powerful genie anything. If he wished for food, the genie could present to him the best dishes from across the world. If he wished for his house to be cleaned, the genie could clean it from top to bottom within seconds. If he wished to travel, the genie could carry him to wherever he wished to go in a fraction of a minute. If he wished for a new home, the genie could manufacture this in a minute. The man had all the resources at his beck and call. Wow. This was bliss. But wait. There was a catch.

The Guru when bestowing this wish also put forth a condition, "The genie is a powerful being and can't be kept idle. The minute the genie is idle, it will devour you."

In his innocence, the man was not concerned. He said, "I have a lot of work that needs to be completed. I want things done not just for myself but for humanity."

The Guru gently enquired, "Are you sure? Will you be able to handle this power?"

The man said, "I'm confident. I know I can handle this genie. I know what all I can accomplish with this powerful resource that I have been gifted with today."

The Guru smiled and gave his blessing that the genie would manifest the next morning. The man happily awaited this momentous occurrence. He was excited and was eagerly waiting for this powerful moment. All the world's resources would be at his fingertips. He would have unheard-of power.

He could accomplish a lot with it. The next morning, the genie appeared and all that was promised occurred. The man had prepared a list of things to accomplish. Within seconds, each task was done and the genie would present itself for the next command.

Over time, the man found it more and more difficult to think of tasks. The genie would accomplish everything he asked within seconds. This included even impossible tasks like getting a particular flower from the other end of the Earth. The man started getting desperate and was sure that he would be devoured by the genie. He finally understood what his Guru was trying to teach him. It's easy to be the recipient of great power but great power needs to have a direction and most important of all... boundaries.

The man ran to his Guru and begged for his guidance. What was the Guru's advice? He said, "Get the genie to erect a tall pole in the garden. Ask the genie to run up and down the pole continuously and only come when he is called for a task. Whenever you need the genie, call for him. Let him accomplish the task at hand and then return to the garden."

Now, substitute this genie with your mind. Now imagine this great mind that all of us have been provided with. The more you allow your mind space and feed it, the more it is going to devour you. The more your mind rules you, the more your energy gets discharged. Have you seen one of those toys that keep clapping or keep rolling? How many batteries does that go through in one day? Your mind is the one item that will utilise all your reserves, your energy, and take over your soul completely if you let it.

The mind on its own does not generate energy. You can compare your mind to a debauched ruler sitting on a high throne expecting entertainment. He always wants to keep things moving. He wants a constant stream of activity and movement. This can be compared to the actual moment when the genie has devoured the man. The moment where the mind is ruling over man. Man himself has no self-control and is at the mercy of his need for movement, excitement and continuous entertainment.

Where is the man in that equation now? At the beck and call of the same resource and power that was created to give him power. Instead of being the master, he has become a slave to his mind.

Whoever has the higher power is the master.

Whoever has the highest energy is the ruler.

If you analyse the activities of your mind, where do you see yourself? Are you one of the multitude, wanting to be entertained like the debauched ruler? Wanting.... more.

- More entertainment
- Shorter content
- Less attention span
- No boredom threshold at all

Our current reality is living in a digital world filled with social media. This excites the mind. Think about it. This suits the mind. It feeds the mind's constant requirement for movement to the T. Now imagine this as the social media and digital world genie. It was created by humans to help you, to make your lives easier, and to make you progress from physical hardships to a life of ease. But what has it done? It is trying to devour you. This genie too, like the genie of the mind, has to be controlled.

What was created for your convenience is now devouring you. It is keeping you in a constant state of flux and movement. It keeps wanting more and wanting it in less time. If not controlled, it will eat you up. To counter this problem and the numerous diseases being caused, people have turned to drugs. Doctors themselves are prescribing drugs for mental illnesses whereas talking was the resolution offered earlier.

Why are drugs doing the rounds these days? They induce a forced quietening of the mind. An unnatural, imposed period of silence, resulting in temporary peace from external disturbances.

Along with everything else why has this too been outsourced?

Where have you gone wrong as a human?

In your quest to achieve more, you have associated achievement with movement. To constantly be in a state of flux. To want more. To absorb more content. To not want to rest. To never ever get bored.

You did achieve all this but at what cost? The cost to self. The cost of exchanging peace for unrest.

The cost of exchanging happiness with exhaustion.

The cost of exchanging joy with strife.

Everywhere you turn everyone is restless. They are searching for the next high. It's not always drugs. It's wanting more.

Moving from home-cooked food to dining out.

Moving from reading books to watching shorts or reels.

Moving from spending time with families and friends to binge-watching

How to incorporate rest for the mind? From a natural rest which is just not possible given the current lifestyle, the world has moved to the forced rest offered by medication and recreational drugs.

Does this sound familiar?

How can you prevent your soul energy from depleting? Start reversing your choices.

- Opt for boredom and enjoy it
- Start enjoying cooking and eating simple food
- Reduce time spent on digital content and start reading books
- Get together with friends and family
- Enjoy playing board games together
- Go for a walk without your earphones
- Sit in the park and observe the greenery around you

What is the result of embracing boredom?

You will start igniting your soul energy and your mind, which has been racing around like an uncontrollable monkey. It will start settling. There are ways for you to increase this soul energy. That will come later. We will be covering this in volume 2 and how you can measure your evolvement journey in volume 3.

First, to start the healing, you need to change your environment. Remove the toxicity from your lifestyle. The effects of the poison will start to ebb slowly but you need to come out of the web of toxins.

How will this benefit you?

As mentioned earlier, at high soul energy levels, you will be earthquake proof, noise proof and future ready. This however is the result or outcome that you can expect.

What are the changes that happen deep within you that create these outcomes?

These are the 3 Cs.

CHAPTER

05

The 3Cs - Certainty, Contentment, Contemplation

The minute you decide to leave the trap or *chakravyuh* that your mind has woven around you, you have started controlling the genie and can harness the energy of your mind into channels that are selected by you.

Your inner soul energy rewards you by slowly gathering itself. This will start reflecting in certain areas of your life. The changes may not happen immediately but you will start noticing certain differences in the behaviours and actions of people around you. Someone whom you had strife with may go out of their way to speak to you or your spouse may show unexpected compassion.

These changes are all external and indicate what is happening within you. When soul energy levels are high, you will start feeling a sense of inner wisdom. You are no longer adrift in the sea of mankind but begin to experience an anchoring. Things that hitherto did not make sense will create their own space within you. You start to understand the cause and effect of all events in your life.

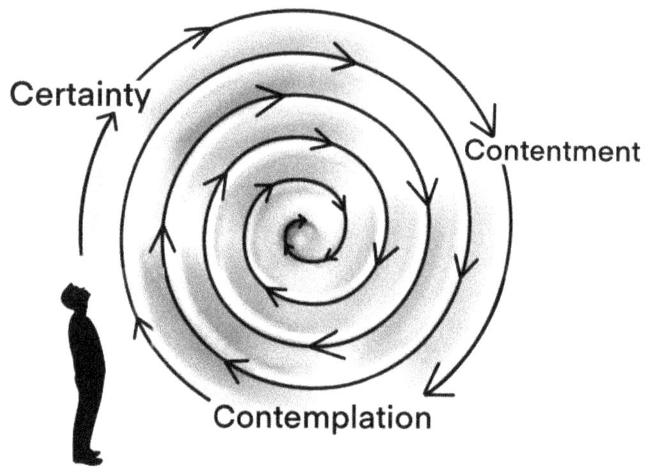

First C of high soul energy - Certainty

The first major change that you will perceive is a sense of certainty. A sense of calmness creeps slowly into you and later permeates into other areas of your life. The source of all teenage strife is internal confusion. Ask any adult if they would like to relive their teenage years and nine times out of 10, the answer will be a strong 'No.' It's because this time of your life was uncertain. You did not have all the answers. It took time, effort, knowledge and experience to gather all this data and add them to the existing knowledge to fully comprehend who and what you are.

The sense of certainty that comes with a high-energy soul cannot be compared to the self-perception that is shared by humans. Your self-perception is not obvious. Look at your reflection in the mirror. What do you see? More than that, how do you perceive yourself? Do you see yourself as fat, ugly, short, or awkward? Your perception of yourself is not necessarily true. This is based on the beliefs that have been created around you.

Have you stared at your reflection in the mirror and hoped to have a better nose or a better figure? I'm reminded of Jennifer Grey, the Hollywood actress who gained fame in the cult movie 'Dirty Dancing'. She was already famous but her self-perception made her want to undergo rhinoplasty. This is a form of plastic surgery focusing on nose alteration. Her decision backfired and her changed looks actually resulted in the loss of her career. In one stroke she lost her celebrity status. She later stated, "I went into the operating room as a celebrity and came out anonymous. It was like being in a witness protection program or being invisible."

Your imperfections create your persona. These imperfections give you your unique identity and create recall in others. When you aim for perfection, you lose your uniqueness. The certainty that comes from high energy centres you and allows for the acceptance of the inner truth. The removal of the stress to be something different creates happiness without conditions.

As a generation, we are constantly struggling with weight issues. I am no different. My self-perception has always been that I am overweight.

From early childhood, my mother and others around me always narrated their versions of how fat I was. My mother's favourite story about my weight as a child was that she couldn't close the buttons at my abdomen and hence she always had to buy dresses for me with sashes to hide this gap. I don't recall any gathering where she has not recounted this story.

This was a belief that was imposed upon me. It coloured my self-perception. As far back as I can remember, I've always perceived myself as being fat. Even when my weight was 58 kg, I felt fat. I felt the same when my weight escalated to 88 kgs. A nostalgic pic of me as a teenager sent by a close friend made me realise that I wasn't fat in that photo.

Why then had I been perceiving myself as fat at such a young age? I realised I had been looking at myself through the lens imposed on me by others. Not just feeling the burden of being fat but always striving to lose weight to regain my self-respect.

My inner journey of raising my soul energy realised a major milestone even in my weight journey. Instead of the struggle to change my body, I developed an appreciation of my body. This body was the vessel gifted to me for my journey in this lifetime and was the only vessel that I could truly call my own. My weight loss and gain journey distanced itself from my self-perception. I realised that my weight was not connected to my identity. My inner happiness was not conditional to my perception of being overweight.

I realised that without raising my soul energy, I would still be adrift deep within. The anchoring that comes with a high-energy soul is diverse from your experience. Furthermore, you might have a multitude of experiences and their associative emotions but with this sense of certainty, you finally start to understand why you went through them and what these were meant to convey to you.

This certainty will start taking effect slowly and keep growing along with the increase in your soul energy. One of my mentees, Anish (name changed), had experienced failures multiple times. He would always attribute these failures to all the fears in his life. In his mind's eye, he was a big failure. All the decisions taken by him were connected to these business-related failures. As he started expanding his soul consciousness and increasing the energy of his soul, he slowly realised that though he had been a hot-headed and impulsive person earlier, he had become patient and resilient now. He shared that he felt a surge of certainty within him. He found a new sense of patience and resilience.

I asked him whether he would like to forget the events associated with his failures and begin anew. The only condition was that he would also have to forego the newfound qualities of patience and resilience. What was his answer? Any guesses? It was a no-nonsense and powerful 'No.' He realised that these experiences were not failures but stepping stones to learning about his patient and resilient side. They were his biggest assets, without which he was as unsure as a teenager. He described his level of patience and resilience as his strengths. They were more precious to him than his failures.

When you have low energy, you focus only on outer circumstances and events or on what the world outside expects you to feel. It's only when your soul energy levels rise that inner truths (that were hidden earlier) take on new meaning and you feel a renewed sense of certainty about yourself. It's a gradual process that is directly proportional to your rise in soul energy.

There have been highly successful people and overachievers across the world who have been trolled, ridiculed and maligned by unsuccessful people. Some names that come to mind are Thomas Edison, Steve Jobs, Dhirubhai Ambani, Jack Maa and recently Elon Musk. Did they change to become one of a crowd? The answer is No. They continued on their journey and took the path that THEY had chosen. The world followed later.

These individuals were all ridiculed at the start and during their journey. However, did this stop them? No. When soul energy levels are high, everyone becomes a Soul Leader. You start to see more than what others around you will ever see in their lifetime. The few people mentioned above and the countless more who have brought about change have this inherent sense of certainty about themselves. They can see more than what others perceive. In today's world, you name this **vision**. Every company is expected to have a **vision** and **mission** to grow.

Soul Leaders are visionaries. I call them Soul Leaders as raising soul energy ignites the leadership trait within. Each one of you can become a soul leader.

Soul Leaders are driven by what they perceive as their inner vision. For them, it's not a risk but a necessity or a path of fire that needs to be undertaken. What seems foolish and beyond crazy to others somehow makes sense to them. Do they care about outside opinions? In most cases, it's a No. They have started something big. They have created something where there was nothing. They have followed their vision. By the time the world starts following them, they have probably moved on to something different.

In many cases, it starts with being aware of what the world needs and working towards a solution. Soul Leaders are not zealots who bring about hate and destruction. They want to bring about a positive change in the world. They focus on products, services, and new technologies that will solve world issues and make life easier. The intention is to provide solutions while seeing beyond what others perceive.

It's only when you feel this sense of certainty that you start to take on the mantle of a leader. You have an inner sense of direction, personal vision and zest to take on the different issues occurring around you and one by one start to seek and implement solutions.

We are limited, not by our abilities, but by our vision.

– Khalil Gibran.

I've always felt the power in this. The ability to see what others cannot is the true quality of a visionary. Working towards achieving this is what creates legends. Others might have visions, but it is Soul Leaders with high soul energy who will work towards bringing that vision to fruition. I was fortunate to read the biography of Jamsetji Tata by R.M. Lala, 'For The Love Of India' some years ago. The love he had for India, his vision and the legacy he left behind still amazes me. He founded the mighty Tata empire. Among other ventures, he founded the Tata Institute of Science. He was responsible for silk still being cultivated in India and not becoming a forgotten fabric. He started India on its Industrial Revolution by establishing the Tata Steel plant at Jamshedpur even at the expense of his health. He started India on its path to hydroelectric power. He gave India its first five-star palace hotel, the Taj Mahal in Mumbai because he could not bear to hear India being ridiculed abroad.

Apart from all that he achieved, which was substantial, what really inspired me was the chapter in the book called 'The Men Jamsetji Built.' Such was his vision that he was able to inspire others and together they set India on a course to greatness. The Tata empire founded by him is still a force to reckon with even a century post his death.

This is the stuff of dreams. You can not only have a personal vision and achieve your dreams by going beyond what others aspire to but also create other strong leaders. Leaders who themselves inspire and achieve greatness. This is the true mark of a Soul Leader and visionary. Their ability to create more leaders with vision.

This is what RM Lala said about Jamsetji Tata, "The purpose came before the men were developed. It was the magnet that drew them. Jamsetji was too big to stop another's growth and the men around him blossomed. The call of his bugle came clear and resounding, and they marched with him. And the march did not stop with his passing away."

All Soul Leaders create something enduring. This can be something small concerning their work or their families, or can be as great as laying the foundation of a nation. There were many incidents in my own life that started unfolding when I started increasing my soul energy. During my HR career, there were many areas where I took a stand and clearly stated that I would like to change something. There were always naysayers and the most common complaint that they made was 'This is not how things are done here.' I agree. However, in my inner vision, I could always see how things should get done. It was so strong that I knew innately what I was recommending would change things for the better. I'm happy to say that once implemented, these projects brought about a transformation in the way things were handled. Processes that used to be manual became automatic. The amount of time and money saved was immense along with the gratitude these projects received from the people who used them. It brought change in their lives. Did the naysaying stop me? Could it stop me? Even when it took months to get approvals and get others on board, it was worth it in the end.

You don't need to lead billions or handle empires to show that you are a Soul Leader. Soul Leaders are leaders wherever they are. And it all starts with this sense of certainty. My Soul Leader journey has given me the capacity to adapt and be courageous. At the age of 47, I left a successful professional career to venture out as a leadership and spiritual guide, mentor, and trainer. Many advised me not to make this bold move. I still wonder at the courage I displayed, but inherently, I was sure that this was the only move ahead. Among all the uncertainties that flooded my life through the change, this inner certainty was my constant companion.

To start your Soul Leadership journey, begin by identifying yourself. Who are you? What do you stand for? What feels right to you? DO NOT EVER take on the convictions of people around you or the convictions imposed on you by others. Always keep a sense of self that is divorced from the multitude around you. You can test what is shared by others but the final decision should always come from within, in line with what you think is the truth.

This truth will evolve over time and so will your sense of certainty.

Do not confuse this certainty with your beliefs. A belief is something that is taught to us. You are trained by others to inculcate a strong sense of belief. A belief does not encourage wisdom and inner answers.

> *"If belief were to become total, man would be finished, because his intelligence would be destroyed. Belief is anti-intelligence. Whenever someone says you should believe what he says, what he is actually saying is that you do not need to walk on your own feet. Whenever someone tells you to have faith, he is saying, 'Why do you need eyes? I have eyes.' "*
>
> *- Osho in 'Three steps to awakening'*

A belief is something that comes from outside and is expected to take root within you.

A certainty is something that starts to unfurl within you and extends to whatever you do.

A belief is something in which others are connecting dots for you.

A certainty is when you start connecting the dots.

A belief is from outside to inside.

A certainty is from inside to outside.

How does this sense of certainty start taking root and keep becoming stronger? It happens when your soul energy levels are high. You also learn how to keep these levels high and not let others take it away from you. Some individuals are born with this attitude. Their sense of certainty supersedes all other influences. They might have been groomed or made to believe certain truths by their parents, by their teachers or other influences. However, they will start to see the chinks in the argument and start feeling their certainty overcoming these beliefs. Then they start standing on their two feet. They know or have a deep sense of inner worth that does not allow beliefs that are foreign to them and imposed by others to muddy their minds.

Is it possible for everyone to start feeling this certainty and increase their soul energy to high levels? Yes. Always yes.

Once you have experienced high soul energy levels, there is no going back. There is no other way to be. Once you have tasted the extra strong shot of black coffee, you cannot settle for the mild variant. Similarly, the zest, the vision, the belief that is the outcome of high soul energy cannot be replaced. You will always want to associate with others who have high soul energy. Others feel like diluted versions. The trolling such individuals face also does not make a difference to them as it becomes obvious that the trollers are hungry for this energy as they have not yet learnt the art of generating or maintaining their energy.

This can be compared to an arena where two different games are being played. Even if the arena is the same, the games are completely different. How can games as diverse as boxing and sprinting be compared? Each athlete will take constructive criticism only from someone who knows the sport. Soul Leaders trust their vision. Their self-identity (*swayam*) is strong. Not all Soul Leaders get recognition. We are all familiar with the history of Nikola Tesla. He did not get the recognition that was his due but he did fulfill his purpose in his lifetime. He moved technological advancement to a higher level and corrected the mistakes made by others.

At high soul energy levels, the need for recognition and appreciation is also less. Such individuals realise that they are ahead of their time. The message or the change they wish to see in their world cannot be just dropped on others. They know that others cannot yet understand this.

Change might not happen in my lifetime.

- Kaifi Azmi.

This does not stop them from executing their vision. Your inner voice will start to reflect this sense of certainty. You will experience a feeling of being more settled.

Let me paint a visual picture for you. People with beliefs are like the blades of wild grass that get pushed around by gusts of wind. If the wind blows east, the blade of grass bends towards the east too. If it blows west, the grass bends westwards too. Wild grasses grow where the land has not been maintained well or properly cultivated. These blades of wild grass find their comfort in crowds. Their identity gets subdued and they take on the identity of the legion.

What is the result of this tendency? All the blades of grass look the same way. They don't have any unique identity. People with beliefs are souls who have gotten overpowered by earthquake souls and subsequently, their inner sense is diminished.

How can you visually represent certainty? Compare this to the mighty tree that is standing beyond the wild grass. A single tree that is visible from miles away. A tree that is affected by the wind but stands tall. A tree whose leaves will show that it is affected by the wind but still manages to be strong. You can count the trees but not the grass. You can stamp on the grass but not on the tree. The loss of a single tree is mourned but the same cannot be said for the grass. The tree stands tall because it knows its worth. It knows that it is a provider and does not take over vacant land.

If given a choice, what would you choose to be in your personal life, a blade of grass or a tree? If you choose to be a tree, stand strong and tall and also provide shade, fruits, and wood for others. You have chosen the path of leaving behind the beliefs imposed by others and finding your inner certainty on your own.

Second C of high soul energy - Contentment

The 3Cs are part of the process. When soul energy levels are elevated and you have also mastered the art of not giving away this energy to others, you will go through all the 3Cs, one by one.

First comes **certainty**. After you have started living your life with this inner certainty and are aware of your inner truth, you feel the beginning of something blissful. Yes, it's **contentment**.

Contentment does not lead to certainty. It cannot be derived only from outside sources. It is an inner feeling. Nothing from outside can ever give you contentment. Happiness can be derived from outside sources but this is temporary. You are hungry, you get the food of your choice and are happy. Your happiness lasts only till you feel hungry again. You go on a vacation and are happy. Once you are back at work, out goes your happiness. You exercise and feel good. You miss your exercises for a couple of days and your happiness disappears. Why is this happiness temporary? Anything that comes from outside and is related to an event is temporary. It is related only to that event.

You have achieved an important milestone—maybe at work or in your personal life. You feel happy and good. It's an emotional high. You feel that you cannot feel better than this. The next instant you are confronted by someone or an issue is highlighted. What does this do to your happiness? Where did that elation, which was just now a part of you, vanish?

As humans, you constantly seek this contentment and happiness from the outside. Others are responsible for your happiness. In relationships, people look for soul mates.

Someone to give you the respect, the love and the abundance that you crave. If your soul does not feel contentment, you will never attract a similar soul.

Do not be that person who is constantly looking at others to guide you, coach you, love you, care for you, value you, appreciate you, and understand you if you do not have these qualities within you. The world is a mirror of what you are inside.

I highly recommend a book called 'A Little Light on the Spiritual Laws' by Diana Cooper. I came across this book in 2001 during a particularly dark phase of my life. It showed me the right path. Conversely, I was seeing the faults of others around me. I was blaming others, namely, my husband at that time. The 'Law of Reflection' in the book opened my eyes. '*Every single person and situation in your life is a mirror of an aspect of you. As within so without. The more a characteristic in someone else bothers you, the more your soul is trying to draw a reflection to your attention.*' I realised that if I was highly bothered by these faults, then the faults lie within me.

A thief can recognise other thieves. A psychopath can recognise other psychopaths. A saint can recognise another saint. What you are from within is reflected in what you see outside. The law of reflection is your best guide to what you need to overcome.

Your soul is like a light bulb that is filled with light. It's actually called *Anand Mayee.* The literal translation is *filled with happiness.* Why then do you not feel this happiness? It's because of all the beliefs that have been stuck onto your bulb. Your light has been dimmed by what others perceive you to be. You have started seeing yourself through their spectacles.

How did this happen? You made it possible by giving others this right. Firstly, by not generating your soul energy, and secondly, by allowing others to steal your energy. What are you left with? A fused bulb that is of no use to you or anyone else. A bulb that does not give light but is looking at others to give it light... Is that of use to anyone?

Start finding this contentment within you. As you gain soul energy, you will start experiencing this contentment deep within.

What's inside comes outside

I've now coached many people who had anger issues. They were always blaming others for their anger. There was no contentment, only anger. Everyone was either incompetent or a nincompoop.

During these sessions, I give them the analogy of a person carrying a bowl of water. I ask what will happen when someone jostles him or her. They answer that the water will spill. Similarly, if someone is carrying a bowl of poison and they are jostled, what will be the result? What they carry gets spilled. I had referred to Jesus earlier. That is my favourite line. Being crucified is the maximum jolt that anyone else can give a person. But what came out? Was it anger or bitterness? No. It was forgiveness.

Father, forgive them; for they know not what they do.

To find your contentment, you need to first take control of your life into your hands. Have you watched television in a group or with your family when the remote control was with someone else? If the channel being viewed was not of your choice, did you not wish to take charge of the remote? Why then should you give control of your life to others?

Before taking any life-changing decisions, increase your soul energy. Start by solving what you see around you. All the faults that you see in the people around you are the reflection of what you need to observe within you. One of the faults that I perceived in someone close to me was that he could not make decisions. Even simple decisions were beyond his scope. He would take everyone's opinions and then analyse them. Even simple things like 'What tasks to accomplish for today' went through the entire evaluation process. This used to frustrate me. I remember using the word 'spineless' in this context. I have realised that when a student is ready, the master appears. The book 'A Little Light on the Spiritual Laws' by Diana Cooper was one of the masters that helped me understand myself. It helped me make the biggest decisions of my life. When I read this book, the first thought that came to me was, "If I am calling someone spineless and it's a reflection of me, am I spineless too?"

I thought about this for days but did not find my answer. I believe that I can make good decisions and I have been content with them. These were small decisions made daily. One day I had my Eureka moment. I was stuck in an emotionally abusive marriage. I was very unhappy and it was getting steadily worse. My marriage was affecting not just my health but also the health and emotional well-being of my son. I had tried just about everything to make the marriage work. I felt I had changed myself to the extent that I could not recognise myself. I had completely changed my inner narrative in the hope that others would be pleased with me. I was seeking happiness from others and this pushed me further and further into a downward spiral. But still, how was I spineless? The realisation came slowly and then it was in front of my eyes. I had allowed all this to happen to me. I was spineless. Furthermore, I was allowing it to still take place because I could not decide to leave this marriage that was hurting me.

I was the first person in my conservative family who opted to break free from her marriage. While my parents were supportive, there were many people in our extended family and community that I had to face. Today I am glad that the old me took this decision. Once I was certain that it was my fault, I knew what to do. Making this decision made my future insecure. However, because this decision was taken with certainty, it brought about an inner contentment as well. Furthermore, there was no question of blaming anyone as I had been responsible for my life and was now responsible for my decision. I felt this same certainty when I left my corporate career. I had been gaining knowledge and slowly building my expertise in different areas but was still clueless as to what options I should finally pursue. However, there was an inner vision that said 'It's time to move on.'

Search for your contentment from within. Start removing all the burdens that you have piled on the poor light bulb of your soul. Unearth your light after removing your burdens, one by one. In the book by Diana Cooper, there is a story of the little soul and the sun. This little soul is confused and does not have any knowledge of who or what she is. The others around her help her out. They tell her,

"You're the light." However, this doesn't help as everywhere that she sees, everyone is the light. The sun knew that for the little soul to realise her self-worth, she needed to see herself from within and not through others. The first step towards finding your inner contentment is finding your certainty. Who are you? Not the one you see through others' eyes but the real you. The you who you know is there within you. No superimposing. To find this inner you, the sun knew that the little soul needed to be surrounded by the opposite of her nature. The sun took pity on the little soul and sent her to a place where there was darkness.

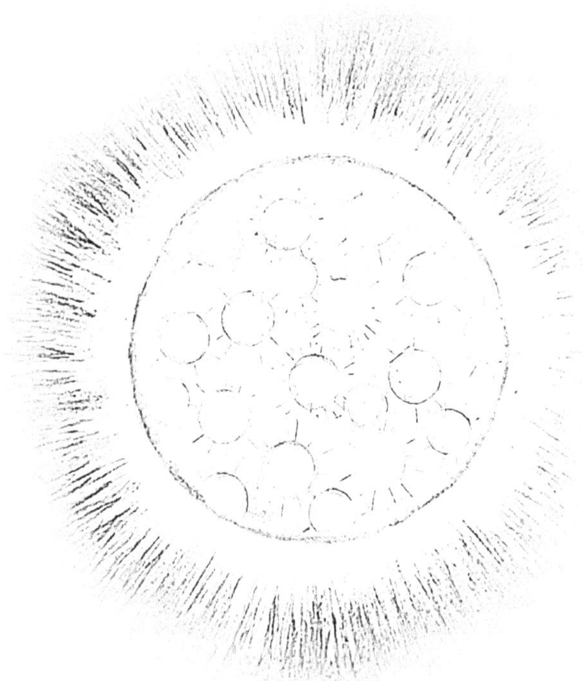

Any place where we do not remember our true selves makes us blind. The darkness here constitutes the life that you all live on Earth. The little soul was born on Earth and had to live the life that all of you live. Since you do not have access to the light or the wisdom of the sun, you remain in the darkness. Surrounded by this darkness, the little soul got disoriented. She could no longer see herself. She reacted to all that she perceived around her, without the wisdom of the sun. She was flooded with hurt, trauma and anger. At the end of her tenure in the darkness, the sun revealed, "Don't forget, you are the light."

This is true for everyone. The more distant you are from God's wisdom, the more you struggle in the darkness. The nearer you are to God and God's wisdom, the more will be your certainty.

Last C that reflects your high soul energy - Contemplation

First, there was **certainty**. This led to **contentment**. A state of contentment then leads to **contemplation**.

Why do you think contemplation arises after contentment? Most individuals will associate contemplation as a by-product of confusion. They think that getting answers that dispel the confusion will lead to contentment.

It's actually the opposite. A soul that is confused, unsure of itself, resonating on a low soul energy vibration cannot be content. Such a soul is a weak soul. A soul that cannot find its way out of its confusion cannot come up with answers. It cannot be the receiver, the radio through which high-energy souls get their answers from the universe.

Each soul is vibrating at its own level. I will be covering these energy vibration levels in the next volume of E-volvement. The process of getting your answers on your own can only happen when the frequency at your end is tranquil. A frequency that is volatile, jagged, and in a state of constant flux cannot become a receiver.

This is similar to a walky-talky. At a time a walky-talky can either send a message or receive it. It cannot do both. My experience of walkie-talkies has only been through the ones shown on celluloid. The speaker adds 'stop' after sending a message. This is an indication for the person on the other end to speak his piece and end with 'stop.'

If a simple message sent through airwaves between only two points needs this rule, then you can imagine the confusion when countless messages are floating around. Your mind needs to be peaceful to receive these messages. You can compare this to a lake. To see your face clearly in the lake water, the water needs to be clean with no waves.

Now compare this with your mind. How clean and wave-free is your mind? High-energy souls hence have to move from certainty to contentment and only then can they become receptors. Being a receptor is an important part of contemplation. Your journey starts with feeling happy, satisfied, and content. It's only when the waves are quiet that you start to think about what is happening around you. You seek answers to questions about the universe and what is happening around you.

See or read the interviews of any great leader. The one thing these leaders will say is how much they like observing others. They talk of sitting quietly in a public place, maybe an airport, and observing others or the chaos around them. They want to understand what makes others tick. What is the reason people behave the way they do? These are questions that arise within them. Their inner voice speaks to them. It guides them and they are satisfied by those answers. This inner silence is also the mark of a great leader.

As a child, one of my favourite pastimes was spinning my *kada* (an iron bangle). As a follower of the Sikh faith, all of us wear the *kada* on our right hands. This is a symbol of our religion. We are made to wear this on our right hand so that if we decide to participate in any negative activity, our eyes will fall on this symbol and it will act as a deterrent. We are not supposed to remove the *kada*. However, I used to like removing and spinning it as it was always fun. What was also fun was to see for how long it would continue to spin without falling. Even the slightest obstacle would stop it from spinning.

Now compare this with your mind. There is a constant spinning happening within. There is a constant state of reaction and you are just like the spinning bangle. Rotating at a breakneck speed. The slightest change in inputs or circumstances stops you mid-way and you fall due to fatigue, exhaustion, and reaction. Can a soul moving so quickly ever receive anything? The slightest change to your circumstances can result in a problem.

When soul energy levels rise, you make this transition. You move towards becoming the peaceful lake from a spinning bangle. You can now go beyond movement into a state of peace. A calm where you do not react to others. Others cannot affect you the way they used to. Your inner calm creates an oasis of peace within. No matter what the world around you is imposing or projecting, your inner contentment causes you to reflect on their words, actions and behaviours, and not become participants.

The word reflection contains the term reflect. Mirrors just reflect your image. They don't let you within. Similarly, when you are in the company of a high-energy soul, their inner silence reflects what they are deep within. Your reaction can be positive or negative and this is decided by your spiritual level.

What does contemplation create within you?

Contemplation gets you connected to all the creative energy of the universe. You enter a state of flow, where ideas flow and innovations happen. This is when you become receptive to what the universe has planned for you. Every one of you has the highest potential to change the world around you. You can make a mark in the world and this can be at a national level, state level, community level or even family level. The size of your influence does not matter. What matters is the change you bring about in your corner of the world. What is the simplest way to measure this? Is it by how many people will cry when you die?

I can relate to this. My maternal grandmother (*nani*) was not a celebrity. She was not known outside our community. However, within it, she made a mark for herself. She was a strong lady. She stood up for what she believed was right.

She was my guide, my mentor, my go-to person. The person who could solve my problems. She supported my decision to opt for a divorce. I wanted to change my name. I felt I deserved a new identity. I wanted to create a better life for myself and my son. My father strongly objected to the name change. My grandmother supported me and asked me to choose wisely. I could change my name only because of her support. She was a great philanthropist. She was generous, religious and much more. She went through a tumultuous life but never let anyone see her tears. She was part of the struggle that took place after the partition of India. She became a widow in her 40s and faced financial loss and fraud within the family. She maintained her dignity throughout. She was the backbone of the family. I was privileged to call her my *nani.*

She set an example during her lifetime but what was surprising to me was this was true even during her death. This was unprecedented and an eye-opener for me. She developed cancer and the last two years of her life were painful. She was stoic throughout. There was a stillness deep within her. You could see she was in pain.

When asked what we could do to help you, her answer always was, "This is my lot to bear. What can you do?"

Maybe I would not have found this unusual if another person in our friends' circle had not been suffering from another terminal illness. My grandmother was calm and bearing her pain soberly, whereas the other sufferer (my friend's mother) used to keep screaming. She was making her caregivers miserable. I specifically recall one incident. My *nani*'s room used to be very hot and sleeping in the same room would give me a headache as I was not used to it. She quietly asked me to sleep in the next room.

She said, "You are young. You need your sleep. You don't need to suffer with me."

When I compared this to my friend's mother, the behavioural difference was too stark to remain unnoticeable. Another incident took place during the last few months of her life. This was when we started praying continuously. The Guru Granth Sahib is the religious book of the Sikhs and also the Guru we pray to. Reading the entire Granth Sahib is considered powerful and is done for all occasions. A continuous reading of the holy book is called *akhand path* and takes 48 hours to complete with multiple people participating in it. A reading that takes place over a week is called *saptah path.* During the last three months of my *nani's* life, a makeshift Gurdwara was set up in her room and the Guru Granth Sahib was placed there. The weekly reading of the book commenced. Now this was difficult for the family to accomplish on their own. I'm not sure how the process started but slowly we started getting volunteers. Even strangers came forward and it started a movement. Everyone wanted to help. People were lining up to come and pray at her deathbed. There was a constant stream of visitors and prayers were also being conducted across different Gurdwaras for her.

The priest from our local Gurdwara who visited commented, "I've never seen something like this happen." He made an announcement at his Gurdwara. "Please visit. You will never see another death like this."

My *nani* was spectacular during her lifetime and pathbreaking even during her death. Her death itself was unusual. An immense peace and stillness settled over the place immediately after she passed on. Everyone stopped crying. You could feel a change in the air. It was a good change.

The doctor who visited her commented, "There would have been someone powerful who came to collect her."

Even after her death, we kept getting information. Multiple *akhand paths* were happening around Mumbai and Punjab for her. Everyone wanted to remember this grand old lady. She made me realise that it's not what happens to you that makes you remarkable, it's how you react to your situation.

How can you bring about change in your world?

At a high soul energy level, contemplation is your biggest companion. It's the reason for all your creativity and the innovation you bring with you. The solutions you provide to everyday problems. Your high soul energy changes how you react to the world around you. When the energy is low, you are in a constant state of reaction. This can take the form of blaming, complaining, whining or anger. It's like all the inputs are coming from the outside to the inside. However, this changes drastically when the soul energy is high. The inputs are now coming in a reverse direction, from the inside to out.

How is this possible? Your soul is now capable of thinking for itself. It's able to take a step back and look at the larger picture. From a micro view, the view gets enlarged to a panoramic view. This view encompasses not just the immediate surroundings and how they concern you but about what is good in the situation. How can it better the lives of not just me but others around me? The low-energy soul views the world from the base of the mountain and can only see what is in front of it due to its blinkered view. The mountain in front of such an individual hides all aspects of the scene from his/her limited viewpoint. This also leads to stubbornness. The more blinkered the view, the more stubborn the individual. Your stubbornness is a key indicator of how limited your view is and how low on energy you actually are.

The higher your soul energy, the higher you can climb. Your view expands. You can now see beyond the initial 50 meters and can start planning accordingly. Your view also encompasses the surrounding areas and what is beneficial for others around you. I've seen this transformation take place multiple times. Just the raising of soul energy changes the entire viewpoint of the person. Their 'contemplation gene' gets activated.

A year ago, I coached Abhinav (name changed) who had major anger issues. The slightest event could set him off. During the discovery call, I realised he was actually someone with a capacity for great spiritual growth. His anger was depleting his energy and not allowing him to rise higher. Even at low soul energy, he was not a bully but was struggling to understand the life around him. He was someone who fought with people at the slightest provocation—on a cricket field and at networking meetings, to name a few. The victim mentality of a low-energy soul was on full display.

A few sessions later, things started coming into perspective. As his soul energy levels rose, this angry young man who used to be baffled by the behaviour of people around him, started gaining wisdom. As a result, his relationship with his family improved. His business started growing. I mentioned him here because a few months after he started raising his soul energy levels and consciously working on this, he faced a traumatic event. His best friend suddenly died at the young age of 34. I remember sitting across from him and listening to him. He told me that he was very upset and shaken to his core. However, in the same session, he started opening up about how he had persuaded his friend to buy a life insurance policy just two years earlier. How he and his wife were visiting his friend's widow and child offering their support. What struck me was his conversation on why he should look out for his friend's child but also not overcompensate him as he would get spoilt.

His high soul energy had not only become the biggest shock absorber but was also guiding him on the way forward. He arrived at all these answers on his own. It was so gratifying to see him looking composed, and handling himself calmly and peacefully. Instead of the tragedy, we spoke about how he could offer his support. The two couples had been close friends. He also sounded surprised by how his wife was still shaken by the event and how it was now his turn to support her.

This was not surprising to me. My mind immediately recollected events from my past. When soul energy levels are high, this directly impacts our ability to understand and process any occurrence. We do it in a completely different way. Where everything was a burden earlier or one more task to handle, things started looking brighter and clearer.

A young client of mine once called me during a panic attack. We had only done one session together. Imagine my surprise when he associated this panic with Post Traumatic Stress Disorder (PTSD). It seemed that a psychologist he had visited earlier had diagnosed him with the condition. I was surprised as there was nothing in his past for him to have developed it. I asked him a few leading questions. It seemed that he had not slept well the last two days due to some urgent project deadlines. I advised him to recharge himself with meditation and go to sleep. He woke up refreshed the next day and all thoughts of PTSD were out of his mind. The label of PTSD was taking him into the victim zone. That day he moved beyond the label and learnt to self-energise. Whenever I've faced any major event in my life, whether it's a failure, a death or even a health issue, I'm always reminded of Joshi Veerji and his words. When faced with an earthquake, the entire world will spin, how quickly you recover depends on your soul energy.

Contemplation does that to you. Contemplation is the mark of someone who has control over their own life. This actually works like a continuous cycle. When soul energy levels rise, certainty gives rise to contentment. This is followed by contemplation. Each cycle of contemplation begets further certainty. This certainty increases contentment and so on.

Some people also associate this contemplation with their inner voice. It's only when you can silence the regular and non-stop chatter of your mind that you begin to hear your inner voice. You start understanding the events happening around you and how you can learn from them. The narrative enforced on you by society and your surroundings comes second to your truth.

You will be surprised by your wisdom and the way you no longer react to the circumstances around you. You then realise that you have reached the level where you are becoming earthquake proof. The earthquake will occur but your ability to understand the reason and to stabilise has gone up considerably. You are still affected by it but you now bounce back faster compared to others around you.

Contemplation does not just cover thinking. It is thinking with an open mind. Being open to outside thoughts but also feeling a realisation deep within. It is this contemplation that lets people make better decisions and be more aware of their surroundings. They are also more open to suggestions but are able to sift through all the noise and realise what is good for them. They are noise proof. An inner impassiveness appears and it brings wisdom with it.

Does this inner contemplation give rise to miracles?

I've shared how an increase in soul energy levels creates a state of flow. Your inner creativity and ability to handle and digest events increase considerably. But what do you think about miracles?

Miracles do happen. Each event feels like a blessing. You receive help from unlikely sources. I have faced some major health issues and I've seen some miraculous healing. I've received job offers that appear out of thin air. I know that this was not my right but blessings were heaped over me. I thank God for each blessing and know that God is with me. I know that I just need to keep elevating my soul energy levels and everything else will fall into place.

Why shouldn't you give advice?

I'm as guilty as anyone. I have this overwhelming instinct to help others. Deep inside me, I feel that I'm supposed to help. I want to solve everyone's problems. If only they would follow my lead, they would really prosper and live amazing lives. But others don't see it my way. What is the gap? What is obvious to me is obscure for others even though it is for their well-being and prosperity.

The answer lies in the 3Cs. I know my certainty and that has led me to my contentment. My contentment has led me to contemplate and search for more answers.

You cannot rush this process. Contentment cannot be gifted where there is no certainty. Contemplation cannot commence where there is no contentment.

You may offer advice from a deep place of contentment. You may assume that your contentment is contagious and it will kick-start things for others. You cannot be farther from the truth. Your contentment is only for you. It comes from all the experiences that lead you to your certainty. Your certainty cannot resolve the uncertainty that exists in others. Your contentment should be used to generate certainty among others.

As Ron Malhotra says, "For change to begin, people need to travel from a state of unconscious incompetence to a state of conscious incompetence."

Don't offer advice. Instead, ask questions that bring awareness. Guiding others only through questions starts their thinking process and makes them aware. It is this awareness that leads to awakening in that specific area and will lead to certainty. A soul that starts this quest based on the 3Cs is now on the path to becoming a Soul Leader.

You don't just ascend this path, you accept the responsibility of becoming a leader in your own life. A Soul Leader.

From never having any expectations from my own life at the beginning of my own Soul Leadership journey, I am amazed at what I have achieved. The activation of my leadership gene happened by default and my increasing levels of certainty have created more of it in my life. Now, I cannot go back to a life filled with uncertainty. This is going to be true for every one of you. If it can happen to me, it can happen to anyone. True Soul Leaders are also able to guide others just by their presence without speaking a word. We will study this further in volume 2. However, I don't encourage this behaviour. It's not sustainable to keep looking outwards for your energy. Become your own source. Your progress will be much faster and you will be the catalyst for your group rather than dependent on others.

What defines people with high soul energy?

I've already mentioned that such individuals become earthquake proof, noise proof, and future ready earlier. These are not just attributes. This is an evolved way of living and thinking. When you trust the universe to look after you, you are essentially creating a protective shield around you. While this protects you from all the insanity around you, it also gives you direction and a sense of purpose. I can vouch for this from my personal experience. I've seen this change happening around me to countless individuals. So I know that it is real and not a fluke. Individuals resonating with a higher soul energy frequency don't have the same reactions as others around them. This is what sets them apart from the crowd, creates powerful leaders, and inspires others.

As per Jack Canfield, the formula for success is Event + Reaction = Outcome.

You cannot start building your home over sinking sand and expect it to stay strong. Similarly, you cannot expect to build your resilience levels after experiencing a trauma in your life. The building of soul energy takes place much before. You start creating the foundation that will stand you in good stead when a trauma or a negative event happens. Your high soul energy levels create an internal buffer against the tough winds. This defines your reaction even if there are problems. Some of these are outlined below.

- You have not gotten the promotion you were working hard for
- You haven't received the raise you were promised
- You have been cheated on
- You are facing health concerns
- You have failed in your business
- You have a failed relationship
- You are getting distanced from people in your life
- You are struggling in your career or your relationships

There can be many reasons. It doesn't matter. It is your reaction to the event that is going to define you and not the event itself. For instance, business gurus are fond of quoting the story about Kodak, where the company was given the first choice to build a digital photography product. The company refused, citing that its current product (photographic films) was good enough. Their employee, who created the innovation, sold his invention to Sony. Sony could foresee the future. It had an adaptive mindset and became the leader.

When I speak about Soul Leadership, I am regularly asked, "Why is leadership a part of spirituality? You can either be a spiritual coach or a leadership coach."

My answer has always been, "It's when you let spirituality into your life that you connect to your inner leader. You start solving all your problems, be it emotional, mental, physical or personal."

Soul Leadership is not just a phrase but a way of being. You start understanding what the universe means to you and what the universe expects from you. Your deeper connection with the universe and your soul gives rise to your inner leadership. The effect of this soul power makes you a leader. You don't need followers to become a leader. You just are.

You start to lead yourself. You are no longer looking outward for guidance. You are guided by your inner voice. You start solving all your problems one by one. The solutions either come to you directly or you start attracting them from your surroundings. Your ability to think out of the box increases. You start getting solutions and incredible answers to problems that baffle others. You are no longer just living for yourself but are someone who adds value to other lives.

It is no coincidence that spiritual leaders around the world have been instrumental in setting up so many institutions like schools, hospitals, not-for-profit organisations and much more.

A Soul Leader is not just a spiritual leader. He or she is not divorced from the world, sacrificing or dedicating his/her life to God. These are individuals who are living amidst everyone. They have the same problems and the same experiences as everyone else. As they slowly increase their soul power, they realise their inner power. They start resonating at a higher frequency level and this activates their leadership qualities.

Anyone can be a Soul Leader. You can be in any profession. A Soul Leader who is a celebrity will last the distance. They will not get bothered by the trolls or the uncertainties of their life. A Soul Leader who works as a corporate professional will lead the way. He/she will create a more harmonious and enterprising work environment. A Soul Leader who is an entrepreneur will create value for others through the work done, the products offered, and the change they bring into their lives.

Soul Leaders will see the future and be future ready.

I've seen a lot of upheaval in my own life. I was always a victim and someone to whom things happened. My discontent with my own life and my choice to always complain was not worthy of my soul. I chose to increase my soul energy and this slowly changed my feelings from within. Decision-making started becoming easier. Even decisions that did not get a positive outcome and in hindsight were wrong were a learning. I could analyse why I had taken that particular decision and why I had attracted those events, people, and circumstances in my life.

Overall my level of inner contentment rose. This brought happiness, peace, and joy. A sense of satisfaction prevailed. Even when I was faced with upheaval in my life, this inner contentment seeped out and I was able to overcome these circumstances.

I have developed an unshakeable belief in God. My faith is not dependent on people, miracles or my surroundings but is based on this inner contentment. I was someone who had many questions. Increasing your soul power and becoming a Soul Leader brings you answers. One day you will realise that there are no further questions. You may have some about your own life and what path you now need to tread but your questions about God, the universe, your soul energy, etc. will be already answered.

CHAPTER

05

How does the Soul Leadership process work?

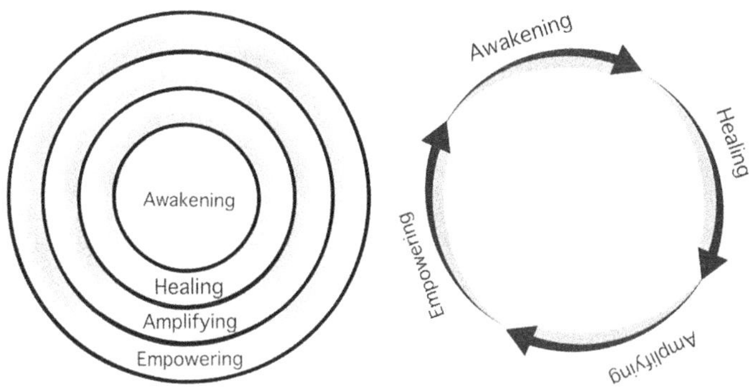

Step 1: Awakening

The first step is **awakening**. Everything starts from awakening or awareness.

You make a change from someone to whom things are happening with no control over any circumstance. People may have behaved badly with you. You may not have received the love and the acceptance you desired. You may have people in your life who are bullying you. You have anger issues. There may be guilt from events that happened long ago that is still clouding your judgement. You change with appropriate mentoring.

During my mentoring sessions, when we go deeper and try to find the source of the problem, the client will come up with events that took place even as far back as 30 or 40 years or more. Their minds have still not forgotten and are still carrying the burden. In one such case, I was coaching an elderly lady. She had relationship issues with everyone close to her. No relationship was happy. Some were better than the others but most of them were discordant. When we delved deeper, we realised that she was overcome with guilt for siding with her grandmother against her mother during her childhood. When we went deeper, it transpired that her mother had been a wise lady and the problem had been with the grandmother. Her alignment with her grandmother had created this guilt which was affecting all her relationships. She could not trust any of them, and as a result, was reacting badly to her present situation. She had alienated everyone close to her. I had to work with her at a deeper level to remove the emotion from her past and after the tears dried up, there was awareness and a resultant awakening.

As humans, you are always imbibing things from your surroundings. You keep scanning your environment and absorbing anything that has emotional value. You don't know where and how this is going to affect you. You might view a violent movie that is stored deep in your mind's recesses. Everything starts piling up. The more the weight of such memories, the more you start deflecting from your current path.

Human beings are the result of their experiences. I've spoken about how strong the mind is. It is very powerful and capable of creating an alternate reality within you.

Be aware of what you are watching. When you start your Soul Leadership journey towards evolvement, you start becoming aware of all that you have absorbed, especially all the negatives that are still swirling somewhere deep within you. What is the best part about awareness? Once you become aware, that lock opens and starts a process of healing within you.

Step 2: Healing

I have mentioned earlier about how the mind processes information and stores all the hurt it gathers like an onion (in layers). Awakening is the key that opens those layers. Opening each layer brings a sigh of relief and with this comes healing. You start realising that what was happening to you at a physical or mental level was not by fluke and was due to what your mind had absorbed. Experiences that we cannot process or that leave a mark on our minds create illness within us.

I remember meeting Radha (name changed) at a social event in 2023. I knew her and we had crossed paths many times earlier. When people hear that you're a spiritual guide and mentor, they open up about their life. Something she said made me curious. When there is unprocessed emotion, it creates an inner burden and that shows in your behaviour and your subsequent actions.

When I questioned her, she opened up about her father. You could see that his death was still unprocessed in her mind and she was choked with emotion while talking about him. She still missed him. You could see that this topic was making her breathing shallow. I realised that she had not allowed herself to grieve and those feelings had affected her breathing.

Any illness takes a minimum of one to fifteen months to reveal itself physically and to become severe enough to affect you. The tenure depends on the seriousness of the illness. Cancer reveals itself between 1.5 years to 2.5 years after the event whereas simple pathological tests will show abnormalities within 1.5 months to 3 months. Breathing issues manifest within 5-6 months after an event.

I asked Radha about when she had lost her father. He died in 2000. I asked her whether she had been suffering from any breathing problems since 2001. She was shocked and replied that she had been suffering from asthma for the last 20 years. You can do the math. No medicine can cure her asthma unless the deep-rooted cause is resolved. You cannot put a band-aid over a boil that is festering. To cure it, the pus needs to be released. This can be cleared and released only with awareness.

Imagine a huge volcano that has not yet erupted. The ground over the volcano still looks normal and firm. But this is an illusion. The lava below is not visible but has created air pressure and changed the environment.

Illnesses can be caused not only by unprocessed emotions but also by absorbing data from your environment. Ancient Hindu philosophy talks of the five *indriyas* or senses that absorb data from your surroundings—eyes (sight), nose (smell or olfactory ability), ears (hearing or auditory faculties), tongue (taste) and skin (touch or sensory function). All these inputs get stored within the huge vault of your mind. The absorption levels are directly dependent on the emotion associated with the event. For example, you were bitten by a mosquito and this has happened many times in the past. Your emotional connection to the mosquito bite will be small. If I ask you after five days, what you remember about that day, you will not recall the bite unless it resulted in malaria. Then you would connect the bite to your illness. Your emotional connection with the event makes you register it deep in your subconscious.

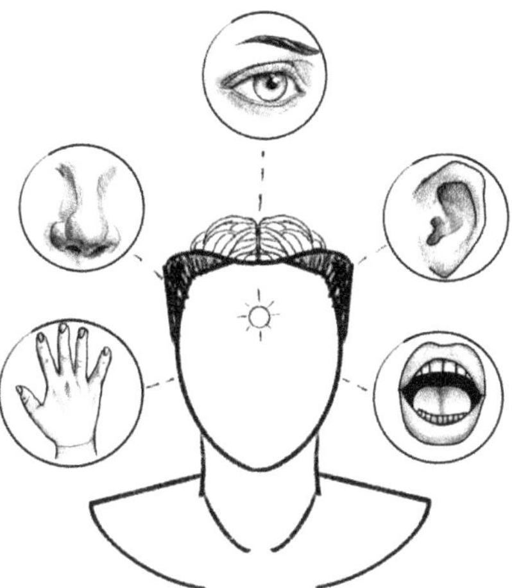

Now think of when you were slapped by a parent. The emotional output from this event will be much higher. It will get stored within your mind and create unconscious associations for you. Your parent might be showering you with love now. But you will still view them with distrust. The minute they start speaking, you switch off. You have built a wall of resistance. When he/she enters a room, you exit. Any topic that triggers the emotion of this event also becomes your cue to switch off. Any abnormal behaviour has a negative and unprocessed emotion connected with it. All such emotions won't necessarily create illnesses. Sometimes, the effects are subtle, in the form of sleeplessness, obsessive-compulsive disorder (OCD), migraines and body pain. You tend to accept them and do not delve deeper due to their non-serious nature.

Imagine a group of 10 people. Each person is given the same mobile phone, of the same brand, model and colour. Now observe the phones after a week. Each phone would have been customised by these individuals and the look and feel of each phone will be completely different. It is the same with everyone. Each experience and your absorption of events from your surroundings is getting recorded within you. This can be connected to family, your friends, your surroundings, or from social media platforms or even from your choices. You will be surprised to note that I have come across cases where it was not something that the person did or experienced, but something that they didn't do.

The most common problem that around 80% of individuals complain about is shoulder pain. Everyone has suffered shoulder pain at some point in their life. The shoulder is the area that reflects all our mental burdens. The left side of your body is related to your feelings and your personal life and is connected to the heart. The right side of your body is connected to your thinking, your professional life and money and is connected to your head and brain.

I recently met someone who suddenly developed excruciating pain in her left shoulder. We calculated when the pain had originated. It went back 4 to 5 months and was connected to the Covid lockdown. She expressed how she had been unable to look after her family and cope with what was happening around her. Her inability to handle the situation gave rise to guilt and this is the biggest creator of illness. She worked on herself and forgave herself for her shortcomings. The pain slowly vanished.

Something similar happened to me in 2019. I joined a startup NBFC (Non-Banking Finance Company) in 2018. The company was associated with a huge financial firm and this was a new venture for them. I was the HR Head and we spent the first year opening branches, hiring employees, and setting up the company. Exactly a year later, we realised there were financial issues within the holding company. As a result, we could no longer run our operations. We had to lay off employees and close down branches. It was a distressing period. Everyone had worked so hard to set up their respective areas. All the branches that had been opened with a lot of fanfare and *puja* had to be dismantled and shut down. Amid this mess, we realised that the admin person in charge of all branches had been feathering his pockets and was fired. The entire administration department was handed over to me along with HR. Anyone who tells you that HR and Admin belong together doesn't know the truth. These are two very different departments, but there was no choice at the time. I had to step up.

The next year was the toughest I had seen. We spent the time renegotiating leases on all the branch properties and closed all the branches one by one. It took an emotional toll on me. The branches, where I had attended *puja* and lit lamps during their inauguration a few months back, were getting their furniture dismantled and sold off as scrap. While we didn't fire anyone, we made everyone aware of the situation and slowly people started taking up new jobs.

Around six to seven months after the news of the fraud, I started experiencing severe pain in my right upper arm. I first experienced it during my yoga class and mistakenly assumed it was a muscle pull. It was later diagnosed as rotator cuff tendonitis. I got treated over the next few months and my movement improved though the pain was constant. The ensuing months were hectic and I could not give myself the time to even think of healing. I just carried on as best I could. I had been practising mind healing but somehow I was not able to figure out the reason behind the pain.

I remember getting massages for this pain and their frequency increased to bi-weekly to help me manage. After nearly eight months of doing this, the first Covid lockdown was announced. I wondered about how I would manage the pain without the massages. However, surprisingly, my pain vanished completely within the first week of lockdown. I then realised that my mind had created this pain to make me aware of my surroundings.

According to Louise Hay, pain in the lower arm denotes that we are handling things that we have the capacity but not the ability to handle. Pain in the upper arm (exactly what I was suffering) indicates that while we have the ability, we don't have the capacity to handle things. As this was on the right side, it was related to my professional life. Can you see the pattern here? There had been an immense burden laid on me. I had handled everything successfully but it left a mark on my mind. The pain was my body's way of telling me that this was not ok.

I completely believe in the philosophy of Louise Hay. She has written multiple books on healing the mind to heal the body. My favourite is 'All is Well.' Please read it to get a deeper understanding of how the mind creates illness within the body.

However, when I mention healing here, I don't just mean healing diseases and pain points. It relates to all areas of your life that you have made septic. In earlier chapters, I've mentioned how the human mind is like an onion and holds onto emotions. Unresolved or negative emotions get locked deep within a particular layer and you perceive the world through these layers. Not all unresolved emotions have created illness. Yet. As evolved humans, you need to begin your evolvement by creating an awakening deep within, one layer at a time, and healing yourselves.

How can you identify the areas of your life that require healing and where the septic emotions have become embedded in the layers of your mind? From your reactions. This has been covered earlier in the book. Please write down all the areas where there is an inner reaction. Certain topics, certain people, and certain events trigger you. The entry of a certain person in your home is your cue to exit. Certain topics cause a mental shutdown.

Why is it important to uncover and heal each layer? Because all these layers have created a heaviness within your mind. When asked about what is troubling them, the most common answer from people was feeling burdened. It's not a physical burden but a psychological one which is due to all the layers of the mind containing all the unresolved and negative emotions and all the heaviness of the past.

How does this translate into your current life? This leaves you incapable of taking on any additional responsibility.

Anyone with so many unresolved and heavy layers cannot be expected to add any more to an already overburdened mind. Should you continue with this kind of life and keep adding onto these layers or take a stand and say 'No More'?

Your evolvement journey will take place by raising your soul energy. We are going to cover the different methods of raising soul energy in detail in volume 2 of the E-volvement series. However, what you can start doing immediately is finding the areas of your life where you are losing your energy. Identify areas which trigger you. Try to temper your reaction. You then realise what you are most prone to react to. You can mentally start visualising your reaction and prepping for the event before it occurs.

You cannot change the behaviour of your parents or siblings. You can however prep yourself to temper your reaction. Your acceptance of their behaviour is your first step towards gaining more control over your own life. It's only when you are always wishing them to behave in a way that is diametrically opposite to their nature that the trouble starts. If you were asked to change your behaviour, would you be comfortable changing it to suit the requirements of your family? If you are not comfortable, how can you expect others to modify their behaviour just to please you? Once you have identified these triggers, you can start calming down. Anticipating these behaviours might actually trigger your funny bone. You can now predict exactly what is coming next.

Have you ever raced a car at high speeds? It takes an expert driver to navigate the vehicle at greater than normal speeds. It is the same with your mind. When the genie of your mind is racing, you are uncontrolled and easily triggered. One of the simple ways in which you can slow down is through meditation. There are many guided meditation videos available on YouTube. Or you can simply sit peacefully and visualise yourself climbing a mountain. Experience the entire climb, step by step, experience your surroundings and see the peak in your mind's eye. Ensure that you do this mental activity slowly, taking a minimum of 20 to 30 minutes to reach the peak. When I started my meditation journey, I would set an alarm for 30 minutes, increasing it as time went on.

Another easy way to engage the mind while slowing it down is to listen to something while doing something physical. This works best for me while driving. I enjoy driving, especially alone. My favourite activity is listening to a spiritual discourse on the car's stereo. While my physical senses are occupied with driving, my ears and mind are connected to the discourse. I do not play a song that I can sing with. That would again get me into an activity mode.

Your mind can either be involved in an activity or listen. Find activities where your body is involved, like running, exercising, cooking, working, and playing some discourses in the background. Your mind starts slowing down to listen to the audio. You change from a movement-seeking aggressor to a passive seeker.

I have found that based on my soul energy level, the speakers over the years have changed. When driving, I have loved listening to Louise Hay, then Brahma Kumaris, Maskeenji, Ishwar Puri and many more.

There are more ways to increase your soul energy and connect your mind and body with your soul. These methods are also aimed at increasing your happiness and peace quotient. These will be covered in greater detail in volume 2 of this book. There is a science behind your soul energy, and it contains physical and metaphysical qualities. It's an entire way of being. I would recommend you don't wait for volume 2 before you start your journey towards healing and raising your soul energy. The above activities will start you on this process.

In volume 3, we will cover how you can identify your soul energy levels. Your behaviours and beliefs are based on them. As you rise spiritually, you can measure your ascension.

You also need to start saving your soul energy. Have you ever tried filling up a leaky bucket? Have you experienced frustration when all your efforts are wasted? While raising your soul energy, you also need to identify the areas and people who are draining you. You need to plug the holes in the leaky bucket.

How can you identify if you are in an energy-draining environment? Identify your levels of control and comfort within your environment. Are you excited and happy with your career? Are you excited to leave home for work daily? Are you similarly excited to come back home? Do you get into a state of flow with your work or does it feel like a never-ending task? This could also be because you have not raised your soul energy levels yet. At low energy levels, each task will be draining.

At high energy levels, you do not get drained by challenges. When you overcome a challenge, it raises energy levels. Was your energy level drained after meeting a particular person or after a particular occurrence? You won't understand how you could be feeling so low. Your coherence levels will decrease. Suddenly, the task is too big to even think of a response. You experience an imbalance within you. You feel an emptiness which you try to compensate for with food, cigarettes, alcohol, drugs, etc. You essentially move your focus from the present and try to reclaim your energy through any means possible.

There are life patterns all around you and you keep reacting to them. When faced with a certain situation, you tend to react in the same way each time even though you know that this approach has been ineffective several times. It's important that such life patterns are identified so you can create an alternative reaction within you.

In essence, stop reacting and start acting. Think of a game plan to deal with this life pattern. How will you act the next time this happens? I learnt how to handle my reactions through my reporting manager. Gayatri Puranik was the Head of Human Resources at JM Financial Services and someone I am grateful to for giving me this power. I remember handling a particular vertical as its HR partner. I had a disagreement with the Head of that business vertical. He was an important stakeholder for me. One day I received a call on the landline from him and he started a tirade. I immediately became defensive and started giving explanations. I was getting worked up and not able to get my point across. I was in victim mode, which was an existing life pattern for me.

Gayatri happened to look up from her desk and saw me struggling. She came over, put her hand on the phone receiver and asked me about the issue. She quickly took charge and asked me to wait for the person to stop talking.

She told me to ask him calmly, "Are you done? May I speak now?"

I still remember my surprise. This was not a go-to reaction for me. I still wanted to get into an argument with him and put forth my point. However, I trusted Gayatri and did as she asked.

I patiently waited for a break in the conversation and asked with a calm I wasn't feeling inside. "Are you done? May I speak now?"

Guess what? He replied, "No. I'm not done," and restarted his rant.

I looked at Gayatri for guidance. She said, "Don't worry. Repeat the same line."

The next time there was a break, I took her advice and repeated the same lines. The business head replied, "No" and hung up. I felt a sense of incompleteness within me. I hadn't put my point across. I was being incorrectly blamed and not given a chance to defend myself. But I still remember Gayatri's words. She said, "Don't let it affect you and don't show him that you're upset the next time you meet. Give him a few days to feel guilty for his behaviour. Your defensive replies will create more defiance within him. You need to show him that this has not affected you in the least. You are above his ranting."

I felt that this was a turning point in my life and I could feel my energy being retained within me. I felt I had gained control over a small part of myself that day. This changed my perspective. I could relate this to the book 'The Celestine Prophecy' mentioned earlier. Instead of reacting as I always did, I had retained control. The next time I met the same Business Head, I was normal. I started the conversation on a completely different topic. I could see him getting baffled and this made me more grateful. I had successfully defeated a bully in my life. One down and more to go. I had been in the habit of feeding my energy to multiple bullies. They would see me as an easy source of energy. One by one, I started regaining control over my life. I stopped reacting.

I would look at the person confronting me calmly and ask, "May I speak now?"

Don't be someone to whom things happen. Make your choice. Choose how you will act and own the event. Own your life. Take back control.

A story I heard from my mother expresses this beautifully. You are all expected to build a bank of good deeds in your lives. This helps you get into heaven. There was a man who was selfish and only concerned with his welfare. He was not completely bad but had not built up his bank of good deeds. One day he encountered a saint. At the saint's behest, the man helped others by giving his time and money. This was not normal for him. The saint was pleased with his service and gave him advice.

The saint said, "There will come a time in your life when you will be asked to choose between heaven and hell. Whatever you might think, I want you to trust me and choose heaven. You might forget my words but at the right time, I give you my word, you will remember them. Always choose heaven."

A few years later, the man died. At the entrance to heaven, he was shown his life's review. As per the review, he was doomed to an eternity in hell. However, as he had shown kindness and helped someone, albeit briefly, he would be entitled to just one day in heaven. He was given the choice to choose whether he first wished to serve his sentence in hell or to experience his brief stay in heaven. He debated the pros and cons of his decision. His one day in heaven would get over quickly and then he would not have anything left to look forward to. However, if he chose hell, he would still have something to look forward to and his days in hell would not seem so bad. As he sat there contemplating, he remembered the words of the saint.

Although he was not too convinced he obeyed and chose to first experience his one day in heaven. The demons from hell accompanied him. He was taken to heaven and left at the doorway. He entered with a heavy heart. He knew this was only temporary and he would have to spend eternity in hell. He moved around heaven but was a visitor and not a participant. The day went by quickly and it was soon time to leave. The demons from hell were calling his name impatiently. Just when he turned towards the exit, the saint who had given him advice appeared and asked him where he was going. The man dejectedly shared his story. The saint stopped him from leaving, saying that demons from hell are not allowed in heaven. While they may roar and rant from outside, they cannot gain access. The saint asked the man to think of the past one day. Had he committed any bad deeds or hurt anyone? Of course not. This was heaven. The saint asked him to sit comfortably in heaven and to keep praying. Bit by bit, he could extend his stay in heaven through his positive choices. The saint told him that once his good deeds and positive thoughts added up, the demons would no longer have any hold on him and would leave.

This story is not just connected to an otherworldly existence but to also the choices humans make every day. You tend to focus more on the negatives and increase their hold on you rather than focus on the positives and increase their weightage. The man's story would have been very different had he chosen to experience hell first. His experiences in hell would have created negative thoughts in him and increased his stay in hell. He would have never been able to end his stay there and move on to heaven for a day.

As above, so below. When faced with a choice, always always choose heaven. Think of all the areas of your life where you could have chosen your reaction, your surroundings or the people around you. Think about this and contemplate, did you choose heaven or hell? It is your choices on Earth that determine your destination. Heaven and hell do not start after you die but are very much a part of your present life. Two people staying in neighbouring houses could be experiencing heaven and hell simultaneously. They are a state of being. If you're happy, content, compassionate, selfless, and caring, you're in heaven. If you are discontent, always whining and blaming others, and being selfish and greedy, you're in hell. I'm not saying that there aren't places and circumstances that are extremely negative and are hell's manifestation on Earth. However, how quickly you recover and make the correct choice is defined by your choices and by your imbibing the right qualities.

The man in the story was also blessed by meeting the saint. He could have chosen to not meet him. There are people in all our lives who are great souls and can take us higher. It is our choice to increase our association with such souls and avoid toxic or negative souls. His choice to meet the saint and his selfless help to the needy created a bank of good deeds. Although small, it gained him entry into a new and positive world. When making any decision, think calmly and always choose heaven. The choice is always yours. Your positive choices will create the positive outcome that you desire.

Another way that you can generate your energy is by being grateful. Close your eyes and list out all the areas of your life that you are grateful for. Being grateful helps you to quickly recover from any occurrence. You might feel all is lost. Instead of focusing on the negatives, you can change your focus to the positives.

Imagine you have a cell phone with all the apps that you need. These apps define your successes and failures. Replace the mobile phone with your life. Observe the apps that you have downloaded into your Gami-Verse. The apps that are now dictating the way you view the world around you and subsequently react. Armed with this knowledge, would you like to have an app that represents failure or would you like to replace it with one that stands for success? It's time to delete the app representing failure and download the apps denoting success. Each day is a choice. Your choices constitute the apps that you have allowed to enter your world.

When dealing with a negative event or a failure, I've found that the easiest way to bounce back is to list down all the things that you have learnt. Did the event teach you forgiveness, patience, self-awareness, and self-respect? Did it make you realise certain fears that you were living with? All these are a part of your awakening process. Once awakened, you can take the next step into healing. Instead of victim mode, you are now analysing each event, and learning from it. You will eventually realise your evolvement levels when you experience gratitude for each awakening.

Step 3: Amplifying

As you let go of your burdens and the mental layers one by one, you start experiencing a lightness in your mind. It's like a breath of fresh air. Everything around you feels brighter and crisper. It's comparable to spring after a harsh winter.

As the soul energy increases and the layers are uncovered, they release pent-up emotion, process the old negative beliefs, and create an open space within your mind. This frees you up and creates more mental capacity. Suddenly the old burdens don't seem too heavy. You start to express yourself better. The right word gets generated at the right time. It's similar to having more space deep within you for more knowledge and learning. More positive thoughts are generated. You find yourself having more compassion and kindness. I like to call this level amplifying. You are actually projecting your new inner peace and happiness onto others and finding the good around you. You have replaced the heaviness and darkness with goodness.

Step 4: Empowering

The cycle of awakening, healing and amplifying is addictive. You now have space for more learning. Your high levels of soul energy are getting you more attuned to God's plan for you. You have a higher decibel level of your inner voice and accordingly, find wisdom in all you undertake.

Decision-making is easier. Your ability to process new inputs and adapt is much higher. There is a higher level of resilience. The failures of yesterday are no longer the end but pose exciting, fun, and intoxicating challenges. You're always happy and see the hand of God in everything you do and everything that happens to you.

Compare this to a small child being carried by a parent. The child is twisting and turning, grabbing at things with no thought of falling since it is secure in the feeling that it is loved and no harm can come its way. Parents are always more concerned with their child's well-being than themselves. The amplifying state similarly gives rise to empowerment. You are now empowered to make better and faster decisions. The insecurity and confusion have given way to certainty. A security that God is close by and looking out for you.

The empowering mode enables you to take risks. You see opportunities around you where others can only see despair. Your ability to rise from failure and be earthquake proof rises exponentially. You may have started your journey thinking like a victim but are now empowered and in control of your life. This mode will also enable you to make long-term decisions rather than short-term ones. This vision creates a future-ready and noise-proof individual who is not afraid of the future. Such people are secure in their beliefs and are able to inspire and motivate others around them. One such person was Jamsetji Tata. I would like to again mention the specific chapter entitled 'The Men Jamsetji Built' in the biography of Jamsetji Tata penned by RM Lala.

I've worked for many years in the Indian corporate sector within the financial services domain. The number of men who are secure in their skin and who create leaders within their team can be counted in hundreds and not thousands. These are few and far between and are a separate species. It takes inner confidence, certainty, future vision, and empowerment to encourage others.

For professionals, the concept of maker and checker is common. The immediate marker that distinguishes an empowered soul from the rest is its ability to take a step back. To be a checker rather than a maker, they need to survey their team continuously and build systems while anticipating future problems.

Painting courtesy - Gaurav Kumar (www.instagram.com/wealthwithgaurav)

I often compare this to Lord Krishna in Mahabharat's Kurukshetra war. He chose to be the *saarthi* (charioteer) for Arjuna rather than commanding the army and being a warrior. In this role, he was able to guide and support the *Pandavas* every step of the way. You can compare this to a modern-day maker checker concept.

Arjuna was a prominent and ferocious warrior who was actively involved; hence a maker. He was someone who handled the activity personally. Lord Krishna, as his *saarthi*, was able to guide Arjuna every step of the way, support him and give him an overview of the war. This constitutes a checker's role.

Now compare this to your leadership skills. Most managers will end up either shouting at their teams, demotivating them, not being able to foresee problems or, in the worst-case scenario, end up doing the job themselves.

This is a maker-level mentality. Cultivating a checker-level mentality doesn't happen in a day. It transpires only when you have devoted the time and applied yourself to grooming your team. Make them strong, empowered, resilient and future-ready so that you can assume the role of checker.

At the Soul Leadership level, when the soul is energised, you start to ignite the qualities of God.

In Hinduism, each *avatar* (incarnation) of Lord Vishnu was measured as per the number of qualities he has mastered. Lord Rama was denoted as having mastery over 14 qualities (14 *kala sampoorn*) with Lord Krishna revered as a master of over 16 qualities (16 *kala sampoorn*).

Each of us has tasks that we have chosen for this lifetime which aim at mastering either one or more of His qualities. Once you have started your Soul Leadership journey and accepted that this is your choice, circumstances and events around you will help you acquire and gain proficiency in these qualities. These qualities can include calmness, peace, love, compassion, self-awareness, forgiveness, dependability, accountability, courage, empathy, kindness, clarity, or becoming a guide.

The Soul Leadership journey will increase your soul power and increase your proficiency level by degrees. You will become a *saarthi* to others. Your ability to foresee the future and plan accordingly will gain traction.

Chess is a game of strategy and involves the ability to predict the number of moves that an opponent can make. Imagine you are in the game of life and can predict and foresee the next four or five steps.

Soul Leadership gives you the ability to envision the end result. Trust God to show you the path to reach your goal along with the strength and the stoicness to not get sucked into the drama around you but to be an observer. You can let others grow, not throttle their individuality, and be at your own creative and innovative best. Just focus on raising your soul energy levels and the rest will fall into place. You will easily move through the four stages and be excited about your progress. Each new stage will bring with it a new understanding.

Furthermore, all four stages of Soul Leadership are interlinked and continuous, where you go from the healing to the empowerment stage slowly. This is not a one-time occurrence but a continuous cycle. Each empowering mode leads to a plateau which is followed by more awakening. After you have been through this process and feel the lightness expanding within, you will welcome each new awakening. You will realise that the empowering stage is bringing with it new ways to be. It includes innovation and a state of flow that is exciting and expands your mind.

Why do I believe in God?

You have been reading a lot about God in this book. I know that in today's day and age, talking about God is seen as old-fashioned. As you've reached the end of this book, I assume you too are a believer but you might have a different definition of God compared to me.

"I want to know, Sir. When will I find God?"

"You have found Him."

"O no, sir, I don't think so!"

My guru was smiling, "I am sure you aren't expecting a venerable personage, adorning a throne in some antiseptic corner of the cosmos! I see, however, that you are imagining that the possession of miraculous powers is knowledge of God. One might have the whole universe and find the Lord still elusive! Spiritual advancement is not measured by one's outward powers, but only by the depth of one's bliss in meditation.

Ever-new joy is God. He is inexhaustible. As you continue your meditation through the years, He will beguile you with an infinite ingenuity. Devotees like yourself who have found the way to God never dream of exchanging Him for any other happiness. He is seductive beyond thought of competition."

The above extract is from the book 'Autobiography of a Yogi' by Paramhansa Yogananda and playfully describes the way most people think of God. This is also similar to how most people describe God. God is perception. Each religion and sect has described God in the manner that God was perceived by them or by the perception of their religious leaders.

My perception of God has not come from just one source but my lifelong quest to find answers to my burning questions about Him. I do not wish for you to blindly believe me as that takes control away from you. That is not what God desires. God is the entity that wants each of His children to travel their path and find Him in their unique way. No two people have ever experienced God the same way. There have been similarities but God lies in the eyes of the beholder.

Another section of the above book describes the reason God has given choice to humans. This is part of the conversation between Sri Paramhansa Yogananda and his guru, Sri Yukteshwar Giri.

"The Creator, in taking infinite pains to shroud with mystery His presence in every atom of creation, could have had but one motive—a sensitive desire that men seek Him only through free will. With what velvet glove of every humility has He not covered the iron hand of omnipotence."

I have come to realise that God is pure light. The nearest comparison that I can think of is that God is made up of light that is *n* times brighter than the sun. The essence of the sun is not just light. It also contains energy which you utilise as solar power. The energy that is being used as heat purifies and creates wellness within you. You cannot do without the healing properties of the sun.

Compare the sun to something more powerful. I'm aware that Greek & Hindu mythologies have associated a human image with the sun. This was a way to explain the concept of the sun to children, a way to simplify and objectify it for the benefit of all the learners. With the advances in science, can you still associate the sun with Apollo in a chariot travelling from the East to the West as per Greek mythology? Similarly, each religion has sought to explain the concept of God. It is also true that nobody was ever able to explain what God was once they united with God, as they lost the ability to communicate and became one with Him.

This is explained beautifully by the Sikh Philosopher Giani Sant Singh Maskeen. He talks about two rocks of salt sitting on the river bank, estimating the depth of the river. Finally, one rock decides to take the plunge. It assures the other rock that it will enter the river, check its depth and return with the answer. The story goes that the other rock is still waiting for its companion to return. However, as we all know, once a rock of salt has entered the river, it becomes one with the river and loses its own identity. It surrenders to the mighty one. It gains the identity of the river. It is similar to the stream of water joining the ocean. You cannot distinguish the drop of water within the stream and definitely not within the vast ocean. The drop of water is happy to belong to something bigger than itself.

The wisdom in the Upanishads, as translated and commented on by Swami Paramananda, states, "*That which comes out of the Infinite Whole must also be infinite; hence the soul is infinite. That is the ocean, we are the drops. So long as the drop remains separate from the ocean, it is small and weak; but when it is one with the ocean, then it has all the strength of the ocean. Similarly, so long as man believes himself to be separate from the Whole, he is helpless; but when he identifies himself with It, then he transcends all weakness and partakes of Its omnipotent qualities.*"

Where can we search for God? I was told growing up that God exists in each one of us. Is God such a small entity that it can be contained within a person? If yes, does God differ from person to person? These were questions that plagued me growing up. How could God that was within me get me help from outside? How could God bring me peace? I now draw the solar system on a piece of paper when asked about the whereabouts of God.

You exist on the planet Earth. I point to the drawing and ask, "Where is God? Can you pinpoint the exact place where you believe God exists?"

Many people have caught the gist and replied that God is the paper. This is putting it simply but it is true. God is the energy that created the solar system. God had to exist before anything else came about. So to answer the question, does God exist within us? No. God is everywhere and all of you exist within God. God is the energy, the fabric of time and space that you exist in. All of you exist within this energy. As such you are all connected. There is nothing in this universe that is isolated and not connected to the whole. It is God's energy that connects us all.

What does this energy contain? Everything. Everything present in our universe has its source in God. Furthermore, God is pure light. This light is filled with energy that emanates pure love. The closer you are to the sun, the more the heat. The more you open yourself to God, the more the love.

"By work, by making the mind steady and by following the prescribed rules given in the Scriptures, a man gains wisdom. By the light of that wisdom, he is able to perceive the Invisible Cause in all visible forms. Therefore the wise man sees Him in every manifested form. They who have a true conception of God are never separated from Him. They exist in Him and He in them"

– *Upanishads.*

Many years ago, I attended a training program by Hemu Karkera. He likened God to a lake. Imagine two fishermen in their separate boats but fishing within the confines of the same lake. Can you think of them as being separate? Are they not connected? Any turbulence created by one will affect the other. Similarly, you are all present in the vast loving energy of God. The distance you maintain from this energy is a testament to yourself and not God.

Each of you is in part an essence of this energy. All of you can love completely. It's when you choose to increase your soul energy that the light within gets stronger. The connection to God inside and outside increases in levels. The farther you get from love, the more distant you are from His energy. You continue to exist within His energy but have created shields that don't allow this energy to enter you. You have built barriers to protect yourself but these have separated you from God, His energy and ultimately love.

What difference can God's energy create within you? What changes can you expect within yourself when you raise your soul energy? In the earlier chapters, we have spoken about the 3Cs—Certainty, Contentment and Contemplation. What also transpires is how you become more genuine. The difference between what you are inside and how you project yourself outside changes. There is more transparency. Your intention and ability to hurt others will decrease. You will start viewing the world through a positive filter. It's actually not a filter but a removal of all the other filters that you applied.

The one thing that all people attuned to God's energy share is how others start perceiving them. Random people will come up to you and start discussing their problems.

Your inner kindness, compassion, and clarity are addictive and attract others to you. This can be compared to a light bulb. Your bulb has started shining brightly. Everyone has an inner light. It's just that others are operating on a lower voltage while some have added too many dark layers over theirs and hence cannot be seen entirely. From just a bulb that gives light, you progress to become an energy transmitter.

I've met many saints and people who are close to God. It's interesting, but do you know that even in saints there are levels? The one thing that transpires even for saints as they grow within their role during their lifetime is keeping silent. The higher their level, the more they take on God's quality of allowing others to choose. They only give hints but do not direct you. Sometimes their responses seem cryptic and you understand what they meant only at a much later stage. This is so because ultimately the choice remains with the individual.

Compare them to the benevolent parent. This parent knows what is good for their child but wishes to encourage the child to seek out his/her path. Their energy stops them from instructing. They will patiently wait for the right moment and drop a hint. They are patient because the transformation they seek in people around them takes place over the years.

I'm not a saint. I am far from being one but I've been around saints and can map my transformation. I was not able to catch these hints earlier and lost many opportunities. I lost hints that I received not just from saints but also from my surroundings. I was too full of myself and this stopped me from receiving the guidance that was given with just a hint.

I'm however highly grateful that I've been chosen to bring you this book. It's not a book written by me but through me. It's a book that was downloaded to my mind and took more than six years to fully reveal itself. While the concept of the book trilogy took six years, it has taken my entire life to accumulate my experiences, all these stories, and my transformation to reach that point where I could be a suitable vessel for the download. Movement in God's universe takes place slowly and patiently, bit by bit. You have to align yourself completely and wait. Patience is another one of God's qualities that you are meant to imbibe. Patience slows down your mind, allowing you to actively receive the download from God's universe. A mind that is resonating at a faster pace misses out on this chance.

Imagine a spinning top. Its movement is mesmerising, but can the top gain anything from its environment? The slightest external stimulus causes it to fall. Now compare this to the pearl-generating oyster. It waits, patiently waits for an irritant to enter and then patiently secretes substances that form one beautiful pearl. There are other elements to this journey, namely, the connections between the Vedas and the raising of our soul energy and how we can measure our spiritual progress. These will be part of volumes 2 and 3.

However, what is the one thing that you can practice that will start you on this path? What is the one thing that God's energy is full of? Love. If you start feeling love for people around you, you are essentially attuning yourself to God's energy and enhancing the process.

All the violence in the world is a result of moving away from God's energy. Everyone who has experienced an NDE (near-death experience) can vouch for the love that they have experienced. I too personally know someone who has experienced an NDE and has repeatedly questioned the experience. I'm surprised why people fight in God's name when that is the farthest thing from God and His energy.

I've been guided all my life to become someone who can experience this and share this knowledge with the world. My entire life feels like a school that I was made to attend even against my choice. I've felt from a very young age that I was made to take birth on Earth against my will. I would dream of when I would return to my actual home with God. I'm correcting you here. I did not have suicidal tendencies. Just an inner certainty that I needed to return to my home.

It's not like I had all the answers and that I had solved all my problems. I had accumulated too much baggage from my previous lifetimes and needed to resolve them one by one. Furthermore, I was scared of this world. I had faced too much adversity in my previous lifetimes and had created a shield around me to prevent further hurt. I wanted to live this life quickly and return home to the safety of God. But I was not allowed to do so. My experiences were lovingly curated by God. Some experiences were loving and peaceful but many were like slaps on my face. There were rude awakenings, health challenges, and bullies in my life. Each experience unfolded a layer that I had created around myself.

I can now look back on my journey and be grateful. I can now understand the flight path that I needed to undertake to reach these heights. I'm amazed at how patiently this life path was revealed and I was given this gift of love.

When faced with a choice in your life or how you would react to a situation, always choose heaven. Choose love. Here is a poem I remember from school. It is 'Abou Ben Adhem' by Leigh Hunt, written in 1834.

Abou Ben Adhem (may his tribe increase!)

Awoke one night from a deep dream of peace,

And saw, within the moonlight in his room,

Making it rich, and like a lily in bloom,

An angel writing in a book of gold:—

Exceeding peace had made Ben Adhem bold,

And to the presence in the room he said,

"What writest thou?"—The vision raised its head,

And with a look made of all sweet accord,

Answered, "The names of those who love the Lord."

"And is mine one?" said Abou. "Nay, not so,"

Replied the angel. Abou spoke more low,

But cheerily still; and said, "I pray thee, then,

Write me as one that loves his fellow men."

The angel wrote, and vanished. The next night

It came again with a great wakening light,

And showed the names whom love of God had blest,

And lo! Ben Adhem's name led all the rest.

This was my first experience. My first step towards becoming what I am today. I'm smiling as I write this. I'm blessed that I was given this chance. My God has been kind. I feel my love for God and God's love for me shining in my life and also guiding others around me. I have long since surrendered to God. I am possessive of God's love. While God is there for everyone, I am selfish enough to think of God as my own. I know too that others have had this similar thought. Sant Kabir or Bhagat Kabir, the 15th century Indian mystic and poet used to call God *mere* Ram (my Ram).

Based on your perception, you will view God as either male or female. There is no gender, decide on whatever makes you connect better. God allows you to create your *avatar* or your version of Him. Something that will make you happy and make you associate better with God.

Also, you will assign God as either being a friend, a parent or a child. Most people perceive God as a parent. A beloved mother or father. God has multiple roles combined into one. I know someone who perceives God as her male child. This is a high state indeed. She is overflowing with motherly love and this is her way of showering God with all the love in her heart.

My perception and association with God are as a friend. A buddy. My companion. I'm never alone. I feel God standing beside me, guiding me, correcting me, and blessing me. My God is male and combines the duty of a friend along with a parent sometimes. He's more of a friend but becomes a father when required.

I had always craved the love of my father. My father was my first experience of a bully. I have long since forgiven him and, in his lifetime, he too requested my forgiveness. What still brings a smile to my face is how God with one stroke showered me with his love as a father. I would always perceive God as a friend and during my meditations hug him and feel love for him.

During one particular meditation session, I had a vision of God, a figure of light, standing at the entrance of heaven, welcoming me. I climbed the steps to heaven quickly and he enfolded me in his arms and lovingly said in Punjabi *'Mere Dhee Aagayee'* (My daughter has arrived). I still feel goosebumps when I recall this. He superimposed himself into my consciousness as a father. Three simple words and I never felt that I lacked a father's love. I'm still overwhelmed by the love I feel for my parent God.

I would like to conclude by saying that I don't have all the answers. However, my inner contentment and certainty have obliterated my questions. I still have a long way to go but look forward to my complete surrender.

Choose heaven. Choose love. Be patient. Keep increasing your soul energy. If you love, you shall receive.

The only way

What has been shared here is the path that I followed. There might be other paths and other ways that you can come up with. What is important here is to assimilate these steps into your own lives and then come up with something that works for you. All of you are seekers and what you come up with can then take this conversation ahead in a way that will shed more light on this path for others. There can be multiple turns on the route, multiple paths and roads, but seek the destination consistently. Keep seeking and keep growing, that is the only way forward. While some of you will reach early, others will do so later. Some might still be active in the old ways but don't worry about them. Look at your path. You are ahead because your time for evolvement is here. They still need to do some growing to be ready for their journey. All of you have not completed your graduation at the same time. Some are still in kindergarten, while others are in school. You are just a little ahead in your journey. It might take others a few more lifetimes. Just be rest assured that their time will also come. God will look after them the same way he is looking after you now. Look at yourself. Start your evolvement journey. Your change may inspire others too.

www.ingramcontent.com/pod-product-compliance
Lightning Source LLC
LaVergne TN
LVHW070031160826
845671LV00008B/244

* 9 7 9 8 8 9 5 8 8 0 2 3 4 *